Get Your S.H.I.P. Together!

The Wealthy Travel Agent Guide to Sales

DAN CHAPPELLE

DEDICATION

To my wife Christy
and all those whose unconditional love and support
help make our lives in this great adventure
called "sales" possible.

CONTENTS

ACKNOWLEDGMENTS

I would not be where I am today without the friendship and guidance of the following people. This is by no means a complete list, and others are mentioned throughout this book.

Chuck Gouge, who taught me the value of building a strong network; Fred Allen, my friend, adventurer, attorney, and a lover of fine scotch; Jerome Alberto, who took me under his wing and taught me the finer points of new-home sales; Charlie Dunwoody, who gave me my first corporate job and became my travel partner as we both changed roles in the industry; Peter Thomson, probably the most decent person I have had the pleasure of knowing and working with; Mike Drever, a true visionary in the retail travel franchise world; the late Bill Courian, who I often butted heads with, but for whom I had the utmost respect; the business owners of the travel consortia Virtuoso, which my agency was a member of for four years—it was from many of them that I really learned the "business of the travel business."

I would be remiss if I did not also mention the tremendous influence the late Gary Brown has had on my career. He took a chance on me when no one else was willing to do so. We were all better for knowing him.

Finally, I must acknowledge the love and support of my family during the ten years as I spent as a business owner and salesman, and another eleven on the road in the corporate world as an industry sales executive. It is because of them I can follow my true passion of helping others achieve success in sales.

Dan
November 2016

www.DanChappelle.com
Dan@Danchappelle.com

Introduction

How did a kid who was raised on an artist commune in the 1970s become a successful travel professional and ultimately Vice President of Travel Agency and International Sales for a leading small-ship luxury cruise line? Well, sometimes I find it hard to believe myself. Like most paths in life, I didn't start out on it—far from it.

I grew up just outside the sleepy college town of Athens, Georgia, where my father was an art professor and my mother was a stay-at-home mom. Our closest neighbor was a half mile away. My folks had started a pottery business, Happy Valley Pottery, and we were the stereotypical starving artist family. Unlike my friends, who went to camp or the lake for the summer, my family spent the summer traveling to art shows in our old butterscotch-yellow Chevy van. It was packed with pots and displays on the bottom and foam mattresses on top for us kids to sleep on. When we drove through the backroads of the south, the vast fields of corn and wheat in the Midwest, and the endless flat roads of west Texas, my eyes were wide open to the opportunities outside our little town. I received two gifts from my parents, the courage to become an entrepreneur and the desire to travel.

I had a little adventure one night on the road. We were driving home from an art show and stopped for gas just outside Greenville, South Carolina. While my dad pumped gas, I woke, got out of the van, and went to the bathroom. I saw fireworks for sale inside the gas station and I made a beeline for them. Fireworks were illegal in Georgia, I was twelve, and what can I say—I liked to blow things up. Unfortunately, neither of my parents noticed I was not asleep on the back seat where they'd left me. I walked out of the gas station to see the tail lights of my parent's van disappear down the interstate on-ramp.

I figured it would only be a few minutes before they noticed and came back, so I spent some time visiting with the attendant. Minutes turned to hours before a state trooper pulled up and asked if I was Danny Chappelle. My parents got all the way to Athens, ninety miles away, before they noticed I was missing. Funny thing, I was never scared. For me the taste of independence was just a big adventure, a game. It is a game I still play today.

Travel, and the curiosity about how other people live around the world, is in my blood. It's probably in yours, too. The business of travel is filled with a number of folks just like you and me. We have a lust for life and the world around us. The difference between us and the rest of the world is that we have learned to monetize our passion. Successfully selling travel allows us the opportunity to pursue life with a wanderlust most people only dream about.

Not long ago, my wife and I were watching Anthony Bourdain, whose travel and food show *Parts Unknown* is one of our favorites. We love his show because he focuses on local experiences and cuisine, away from the typical tourist areas. As I watched him, I was envious. He is what we all want to be on some level, a professional traveler.

So I did something that I have not done in years. I took a vacation for the sake of travel rather than business. My wife and I went to places that, in all of my career visiting exotic destinations such as London, Sydney, and Cleveland, I have never been. I was struck by how fortunate we are to be in a business that allows for such wonderful opportunities to visit other countries and cultures. Seeing travel again, viewed through the wide-open eyes of a vacationing traveler, was a mind-blowing experience for me.

Whatever we choose to call ourselves—travel agent, travel adviser, or travel professional—we all have one thing in common. We are all purveyors of the travel experience. We help create irreplaceable memories for our clients. For some, it may be their very first Carnival cruise, while for others it is a trip to the Arctic to see polar bears. We must never forget that we are an important component to their travel experience.

> *"Do not let making a living prevent you from making a life."*
> —John Wooden

WHO IS THE WEALTHY TRAVEL AGENT?

I am often asked this question. The answer is quite simple—and usually not what most people assume.

People often and incorrectly assume the Wealthy Travel Agent is exclusively focused on selling affluent travel. It's not, although this is an important part of the overall sales strategy. Being a WTA is about you becoming who and what you want to be, pursuing the life you want to live, and having the means to do so.

Toward the end of *Sabrina*, the classic movie about a wealthy family and their son who falls for the chauffeur's daughter, the chauffeur is revealed to be a millionaire. He's asked how he could possibly have accumulated that much money on a chauffeur's salary. His response? He listened in on his boss's business dealings in the car. "I paid attention. When he bought, I bought. When he sold, I sold."

The chauffeur became wealthy by paying attention to the actions and adopting the mindset of a very successful man. This book will show you how to do the same. There are a number of very successful people selling travel and there will be many more in the future. Will you be one of them?

The Wealthy Travel Agent is a mindset that travel professionals should adopt to become strong, profitable, independent business people. Whether you work in brick-and-mortar travel stores or are home-based independent contractors (ICs), you must remember what business we are really in. We are all in the retail sales business and I will remind you of this throughout the book. We happen to have a wide range of really cool products to sell. Let's face it, we could be selling nuts and bolts, but we chose to sell travel.

Success is all about the choices you make. One of the most important choices is to treat your business for what it really is: a business, not a hobby. If you aren't willing to make that commitment, I will happily give you your money back for this book. Otherwise, this book is a big step on the incredible journey toward the life you want to be living.

Don't listen to the naysayers—they are out there. They are jealous of the success of others. This a profession in which anyone can make a great living and a great life, and even become a "citizen of the world" like my good friend Peter Thomson has chosen. If a dirt-poor hippie kid and college dropout like me can do it—so can you! However, there are no trophies for participation or mediocrity. As professionals, we are entrusted with one of the most valuable things in a person's life, their vacation.

They'll remember their vacations forever, so we owe it to our customers and ourselves not to screw it up.

CREATING A PERSONAL POWER PORTFOLIO

In 2015, I proudly watched as my parents received the Georgia Governor's Award in the Arts & Humanities. They were recognized because of their incredible contribution to the arts in the state. Now, they didn't receive this award because they made the single best piece of art. Nor was it because they sold a piece of pottery for the highest price. It wasn't because they are amazing teachers or because they're the founders of a thriving art commune or because they're hardworking business owners, although they're all those things. The governor didn't value their contribution to the arts because of one single accomplishment or skill. It was their entire portfolio of work, as well as the experiences and skills that they personally embody—what I like to call their "power portfolio."

When they were driving around in that old Chevy van, selling their work at shows all over the country, they were adding to that portfolio. When they were taking risks with their art and their business, they were adding to that portfolio. When they were teaching others—you got it—they were adding to that portfolio. For over forty-five years, my parents kept their heads down, focused on growing their pottery business, and never stopped believing in themselves. Even when we had tuna casserole for Thanksgiving dinner because we couldn't afford a turkey, they never stopped believing in themselves.

This kind of self-belief is responsible for much of my success in business and life. I know that when I keep my head down and add skills and experiences to my power portfolio, I increase my value—to myself, to my family, and to my clients. I don't have to worry that I'm worth my salary or commissions when I know that I bring value to a transaction.

Much of the content in this book is based on my own personal experience. My specialty is selling to affluent travelers and this will be referenced throughout the book. However, these lessons can be applied to any segment and prospect type you on which choose to focus your sales efforts.

The purpose of this book is to help you create your own unique power portfolio. It is about creating value in you. I often hear sales professionals complain that they are not being paid what they think they are really worth. If this is the case for you, you have come to the right place. By the time you complete this book, you will be better equipped to demand a higher salary, higher fees, and working conditions that best suit your lifestyle. Why? Because continuous learning, investing in yourself, and believing in yourself are keys to achieving success—not as defined by society, but as you define it.

Selling is the business you have chosen, so the first place to start is creating value in you at the personal level. Investing in your own specialized knowledge and skill base via self-study, coaching, and training programs will increase your market value tremendously. In an industry where the hobbyists far outnumber the qualified professionals, you will be in a position negotiate a higher salary package or higher fees for your services. Simply put, you are creating a demand for yourself.

Next, you create value for your business or employer. Companies must make a profit to survive. This means that the more profitable your sales are, the more valuable you are to the business. Business flows in cycles. The higher your sales volume and margins on the products you sell, the more likely that you will not be the one downsized in the next recession. You become too valuable to let go.

Finally, you will create value to the customer. These days, the customer is bombarded with purchase options. The key is to get them to buy from you, not based on price, but on the value and expertise you bring to the transaction, with the goal of creating a long-term relationship.

Bottom line—your compensation, whether as an employee, independent contractor, or business owner, is directly related to the knowledge, skills, and relationships you acquire. This is your power portfolio!

THE KEY CONCEPTS

In this book, I will focus on the five areas you need to master to be successful in travel sales:

1. *The Opportunity*—why the next twenty years are the best time in the history of the world to be involved in travel and tourism sales.
2. *The Wealthy Travel Agent Mindset*—how to get your S.H.I.P. together, build confidence, and set goals.
3. *The Business of the Travel Business*—how to make money selling travel.
4. *The Wealthy Travel Agent Sales System*—from prospecting to follow up, a complete roadmap you can use starting right now.
5. *Why Travel Agents Fail*—a primer on the pitfalls and how you can avoid them.

CALL TO ACTION

To get the most out of this book, I ask you to do a few things:

Keep an open mind. You will notice many of the suggestions I make are contrary to standard operating procedure. This is because to stand out from the crowd, you will need to do things differently. Many of the practices I prescribe are commonplace in other commission-sales professions, but for one reason or another they haven't made it into the accepted norms of travel and tourism sales.

Be brutally honest with yourself. The only way you can change or improve behavior is to be truthful about what you are changing. This may be difficult, especially if someone has been blowing smoke up your ass for a while about how great you are. Get feedback from people you trust. Have them review the exercises that are a part of this book. If they tell you everything is good, with nothing to change or improve, find someone else who will be as honest with you as I am asking you to be with yourself.

Take notes. This book is meant to serve more as a textbook than a summer read. Write on the pages, highlight sentences. Refer to the book and your notes often. If you find it sitting on the shelf for an extended period of time, please give it to someone who will use it.

Take the ideas and concepts and use them. Most people are not willing to implement what they learn and they get no results—don't be one of those people! While this book contains systems and processes that have worked for me and many others, please do not interpret anything as an income claim or guarantee that you will get the same results. The only thing I can guarantee is that nothing will happen for you unless you take action on what you learn.

Now, let's get this party started!

Chapter 1
Opportunity

"The business of experiential luxuries remains largely one based on paying full list price. Luxury travel is the only widely discounted experiential luxury."
—Pam Danziger, Unity Marketing Group

Why are consumers willing to pay full price for dining, theater tickets, and even housekeeping services, but not for travel? Based on my observation and experience, the answer is simple. The travel trade does not effectively communicate its value to the consumer. The majority of travel professionals sell based on price. Very few have a proactive, value-based sales strategy—here lies the opportunity.

Most travel agencies in today's market will sell to the consumer anything and everything they can. After all, they can sell virtually any product on the market. This means a cruise, tour, hotel, air ticket, bus pass, rail pass, you name it—they can sell it. But should they?

The surprising answer is *no*! You might expect that a business with the widest range of offerings would be the most profitable, but in fact the highest financial rewards come from narrowing the field to specific travel products or destinations. The benefits are obvious. The average contemporary product sells for around $2000, with a commission of only $260, while niche and luxury products sell for an average of $10,000, and the commission checks come with commas. The problem is that most travel professionals do not have a proactive strategy to become the go-to expert for these higher-commission products.

You know what really ticks me off? It's when travel agents tell me they can't sell a luxury or niche product, or even worse, that they don't have "those" clients. I hope you aren't thinking that right now. That's BS! Everyone has these clients, and anyone who takes a little time to educate themselves can sell those products.

Did you know that the higher the price point or more unique a product is, the greater the percent of bookings that are direct? It's true, but contrary to popular belief, most suppliers are not out actively soliciting the public to book with them directly. It's actually because there are not enough travel agents not selling the products.

Whether a cruise or a tour, these luxury and niche products are typically at full capacity. Most of these companies do not have the resources to proactively recruit direct business, which means if agents are not selling the products, then the client must be reaching out to the supplier to buy them. As a sales channel, most travel professionals are so focused on the name-brand cruise and tour companies that, for the most part, they tend to ignore the rest.

Frankly, this is to be expected. Companies such as Carnival, Viking River Cruises, Royal Caribbean, and Perillo all have a higher profile and greater brand awareness with both agents and consumers. These are brands you frequently see on television. They also happen to be the same products every other travel professional in the world is selling, so the competition is pretty stiff. But what do you think would happen if you started offering some of the lesser-known, up-market products like specialty river and small-ship cruises or expedition trips to your clients?

Your clients will buy what you sell them. If all you offer are mass- and premium-market products, then that's all they will buy—from you. My guess is that you probably haven't told them you sell anything else. So why should you expect them to buy their river cruise, safari, or trip to Machu Picchu from you? Based on what you market, all they think you sell are huge ocean-going theme parks and bus tours. Your clients are buying these other vacations. They are either purchasing from a travel professional who is a specialist in that product or destination, or worse— they are booking direct.

UNDERSTANDING MARKET SEGMENTS

These days, you can't turn around in a port-a-potty without hearing about Millennials. They're all the consumer and trade media talk about. I don't know about you, but I am tired of hearing about them. The media goes on and on about how they are so much different than any other generation. Heck, that's what they said about Baby Boomers.

I am going to let you in on one of the biggest secrets in the travel industry. Are you ready?

To become a WTA, you should not be looking at Millennials as your target customers. Don't worry about them. In time, they'll be some of your best prospects—there is plenty of data to back this up. The challenge with Millennials is twofold and will be constant for the next fifteen to twenty years: they are busy working and raising kids.

The big opportunity is the Baby Boomer generation, those born between 1946 and 1964. According to Northern Trust, a wealth management firm based in Chicago, Boomers represent nearly 50 percent of the discretionary spending in the marketplace, and their number one interest is "travel." At the Crystal Cruises 2016 meeting for top producers, former CEO Edie Rodriguez reported that Baby Boomer spending has overtaken that of their parents' generation for the first time in company history. I was born in 1964, the last year of the Boomers, and based on my experience, we are just coming into our own. Here's why.

By 2018 there will be approximately 76 million Baby Boomers over the age of fifty-three and they will be in their prime travel years. Their kids are grown and gone, careers are winding down. They have a nice nest egg in the form of home equity, 401k, savings, and other investments. They will also have plenty of time to travel and do the things they enjoy. They are young at heart! Did I mention that less than 10 percent of consumer marketing, with the exception of pharmaceuticals, is targeting Baby Boomers? I think this is a huge opportunity for travel sales and marketing.

Millennials, on the other hand, are in the midst of their careers, with kids in school, large mortgages, and hefty student loans to pay off. They currently do not have the resources to travel in an affluent manner. But I will share this—they will! If you build connections with them now, you may reap major rewards in a decade or two.

Of course we are forgetting about one important group of people. They have as much buying power as the Boomers, yet everyone seems to have forgotten about them. If my grandparents are from the Greatest Generation, my younger sister hails from the Forgotten Generation, or as we lovingly refer to them—Gen X. While not as large in numbers as the Boomers, they are following right behind them and could extend the Boomer sales opportunity by five or more years.

LEVERAGING INDUSTRY GROWTH

The industry has a tremendous opportunity ahead. New products are coming to the market, tried-and-true brands are evolving to meet the demands of modern customers, and existing markets are expanding their capacities. The luxury cruise market increased its capacity by 45 percent in 2016 alone. The figures underscore the need for qualified travel professionals to cater to the affluent traveler.

Let's be real—you can't just hang out a shingle and announce to the world that you are in the travel business or catering to the affluent traveler. In the pages that follow, I will show you who luxury travelers really are, how to find them, and take the mystery out of selling to the affluent traveler. These are the very profitable clients you want for your business, and it's easier to find them than you might think!

If you question the demand, just look at what Crystal Cruises has done in the past few years. They have introduced private jets, yachts, and river cruises to complement their fleet of large luxury ships. Crystal and other suppliers have figured it out and are keeping up with the demand for their brands. Now it's up to us to sell all of these new products!

Whether you are new to the industry or a seasoned pro, there will be enough business for everyone. Stay focused on what you can do and don't worry about your competitors. It all starts with a Wealthy Travel Agent mindset.

Chapter 2
The Mindset of
a Wealthy Travel Agent

What is this WTA mindset I keep talking about? It's a unique approach that you should take to stay focused on achieving maximum success in your business. In this section I'll talk about what the WTA mindset entails and how you can master it. First, you'll need to get your S.H.I.P. together!

GETTING YOUR S.H.I.P. TOGETHER

What's your S.H.I.P. and why do you need to get it together? S.H.I.P. stands for Skills, Habits, Inspiration, and Performance and Planning. Once you have built and strengthened those four areas, you can master the Wealthy Travel Agent mindset and achieve success even in a stormy economy. Think of your customers as passengers on your S.H.I.P. They won't get on board unless they can tell you have your S.H.I.P. together!

Skills

It is important to remember what business we are in. You are not in the "travel" business, even though we refer to it that way sometimes. Travel is the product you sell. You are not in the cruise or tour business—that's what companies such as Seabourn and Tauck do. You are in the retail sales business. The required skills are in the areas of relationship building and sales. In my mind the relationship skills are as important as sales skills for one simple reason. Your selling skills will get you the buyer. Your relationship skills will get the client to come back for their next vacation and the ones after. The strength of these relationships can also lead to referrals. Your prospecting skills will keep the funnel full, but relationships you nurture will help to ensure that you're still in business next year.

That said, some relationships may not convert to sales right away. You have to strike a balance between selling now and selling down the road. What good are you to those long-term customers if you go out of business before they're ready to buy? In order to increase your value to your customers (and thus your compensation), you must learn to become a successful salesperson.

So what are the secrets to becoming a top salesperson? All top salespeople have three things in common:

1. They practice the fundamentals of their profession.
2. They have complete confidence in their knowledge and abilities.
3. They have systematic processes.

Is it really that simple? Of course not. It takes considerable time and preparation to master the fundamentals. It may seem boring or low-level to practice sales fundamentals, but they are far more effective in converting prospects into clients than some shiny bells-and-whistles marketing gimmicks.

Don't believe me? Look at virtually any competitive sport. I played football throughout my middle and high school years. Many of my high school coaches were the same ones from middle school so I learned their techniques early as the fundamentals of my position. I was ok, but not great. I hovered between first and second string most of my high school years.

For my senior year, I transferred to a school in a neighboring county. I went from a 2A school with homemade weight benches and a football field that was used for multiple sports to a 4A school with a gymnasium-sized weight room and a dedicated practice field—not to mention the stadium! The athletic programs could not have been more different, not just in the facilities, but also in the quality of coaching. At the smaller school, we went spent 75 percent of the time scrimmaging and 25 percent on the fundamentals. At the larger school that had won multiple state championships, 80 percent of the time was spent learning and practicing the basic fundamentals of the game. Blocking, tackling, passing, catching. But it went beyond that. Football is a grueling sport so a player must have the strength, speed, and endurance. Physical conditioning is considered a key fundamental. Needless to say, almost everything I had learned since middle school had to be relearned. I rode the bench that final year, but I learned an important lesson about playing the game at a high level.

The lesson? You can't play the game, any game, and win consistently if you don't have the core fundamentals down pat. I learned this lesson in high school football and have applied it in other areas of my life—especially sales. I did not become a good salesperson because I was naturally talented. In fact, just the opposite is true. I worked—and I worked hard—to learn and master the fundamentals of sales.

Habits

Habits train your mind for success. Let's start by dispelling a myth popularized by success gurus from Zig Ziglar to Tony Robbins and everyone in between. Contrary to popular belief, it does not take three weeks to form a habit. This misconception came about after Dr. Maxwell Maltz, an American cosmetic surgeon and author of the 1960's bestseller *Psycho-Cybernetics*, noticed that it took twenty-one days for amputees to stop **feeling phantom sensations** in an amputated limb. In other words, the person accepted the fact that the limb was gone and not coming back. He then theorized based on this observation that it took twenty-one days to create a new habit or break an old one. Since then the "21-Day Habit Theory" has become an accepted part of virtually every self-help program on the market. The problem is that there is no evidence to support this theory. In fact, subsequent studies have shown that, depending on the complexity of habit being formed, it can take as little as eighteen days to as long as a year or more. But the average time is about six weeks.

Now the good news! It's really up to you how long a habit takes to form, and there are ways to shorten the process and make habits stick. As human beings, we have only two things that motivate us: *pain* and *pleasure*. Known in psychology as the primary motivators, they influence everything we do. Consciously associating pain or pleasure with an activity can affect the time it takes to learn a new habit or routine.

For example, most salespeople associate prospecting, the process of finding new customers, with pain. It is the pain of rejection that they fear and tend to internalize. But what if that same activity were associated with pleasure? It would become something they'd look forward to! In fact, they might even do it every day—until it becomes a habit.

So how do you turn a pain into a pleasure? In this case, associating prospecting with the pleasure of having money to pay the bills, go to the movies, or buy a new car can be greater than the pain of rejection. Over time, the pleasure of having money as a tool to get what you want overrides the fear of not having it.

> *"We are what we repeatedly do.*
> *Excellence, then, is not an act but a habit."*
> —Aristotle

The role habits play in your day-to-day success is enormous. Some authors, myself included, have a hard time sitting down and writing. I am driven by process, but recording that process on paper is another story. I consider myself a poor typist—my technique is more of a hunt-and-peck style. I will do everything I can to keep from sitting down and typing a paper or a speech. I associate considerable pain with this process because it takes so long to produce my work. This is commonly known as procrastination (a habit I am sure you've never heard of). I have tried dictating to voice recognition software, writing by hand on countless legal pads, and many other strategies to avoid typing—but at the end of the day, the material still has to get from my brain to the computer. As much as I dislike it, I force myself to do this. I've been told many times that I've probably forgotten more about what it takes to build a successful travel sales business than most people learn in a lifetime, and maybe they are right, but only because I have made it my life's work to study why people buy and how they spend their discretionary dollars. I have so much knowledge in my head—the one place it really does nobody any good. That's why I'm developing a habit to achieve my goal of writing this book.

How am I doing it? I am biting off little pieces at a time. Basically, I've broken up my big goal into many small goals that translate into daily habits. One of them is writing 2000 words a day. I don't make it to 2000 words every day, but I do write every day, and herein lies the magic. While I may not achieve my exact daily word target, I am creating the habit of writing every day. I accomplished this by associating the habit with a huge positive outcome. And you know what? You are reading this, so it is working!

If you're trying to accomplish a big goal like writing a book or running a marathon, break it down into small daily habits. If you're trying to motivate yourself to do smaller, more mundane tasks, think about your bigger goals and how those tasks will help you get there.

Most salespeople detest calling prospects. They associate the prospecting process with telemarketing and rejection. Having been on the receiving end of many telemarketing calls, I can see why people hate making them. But if my travel agent were calling with the latest promotion for a trip I wanted to take, well, that's a different story. So a negative association with prospecting, whether that's being hung up on or having doors slammed in your face, means you should either change the association or find another line of work. We are in the sales business and prospecting is part of the process. Prospecting should be about finding the *yeses*, not internalizing the *nos*.

Now, if your association with prospecting is that it brings sales opportunities, which will provide the income to send a kid to college, put food on the table, and pay the bills, you will have a positive association and look forward to the practice. Best case—you'll realize that you are doing the prospect an injustice by not regularly reaching out to them. What if the prospect misses out on a dream vacation because you were too negative to make the call?

Set a daily prospecting target with the goal of forming a new habit. You may set a target of ten prospect calls a day but only make three. That's OK. The important thing is that you are building the habit of making those calls each day.

Develop rituals

There's another type of habit that can have a positive impact on your life and work: the personal ritual. Rituals help you establish triggers that put you in the same state of mind and body each time you start a particular activity. Actors are probably the most proficient practitioners of rituals. Think about it—they have to create an artificial state of mind and body that is believable to you and me in the audience. If a scene calls for the actors to cry, most have a ritual to conjure the tears. They may relive a hurtful experience, remember the death of a loved one, or recite a sad piece of poetry in their head. The result triggers an emotional response and the actor cries on cue. The actor Jack Lemmon had a ritual of saying the words "magic time" before he went on stage. This was his cue to become the character.

Baseball players are notorious for their pitching and at-bat rituals. They do the exact same thing every time they throw a pitch or step into the batter's box. These carefully crafted rituals are designed to place them in a state of mind and body that will result in the perfect pitch or the perfect swing. Former Red Sox third baseman Wade Boggs was famous for his rituals: he ran wind sprints at exactly 7:17 p.m. and ate chicken before every game. Did the chicken help him catch ground balls? Probably not, but completing the rituals helped Boggs get into the state of mind to play a good game of ball.

What is it that gets you into a great state of mind, one that empowers you to go out and conquer what the world has to offer each day? My ritual, believe it or not, is singing a stupid, stupid song that I learned over thirty years ago at sales school in Nashville,

Tennessee. It's called "The Bookman's Song," and I repeat, it is so stupid, but it helps get me into a positive state each day. It is happy and high energy, and when I sing it in the shower (my wife has been known to throw cold water to shut me up), I feel great and ready for the day. I have other rituals for particular things, like listening to certain songs and reciting inspirational quotes. Each ritual is designed to get me in the best frame of mind for a specific task. Rituals are different for each person. Whatever yours are, they need to be personal and internalized to effectively get you into the state where you can perform at your best.

You may be nodding your head in agreement at this point. You already know the habits and rituals you need to master to gain success. If so—great! But if you're scratching your head and wondering how to even decide which habits to develop, don't worry. I'm going to share with you the easiest and fastest way to become successful.

Emulate successful people

Seek out individuals who have achieved a level of sales or business success that you want to achieve and emulate or copy what they have done. They can help you avoid the mistakes they have already made and learned from. Well, Dan, that's easy for you to say. You've been successful in many areas of the travel business. To that I say—yes, I have been! Thank you!

But that's not the end of the story. I would have never achieved what I have without taking one very important action: I sought out people who I viewed as successful. I wanted to know how they got to where they were in their business. I observed their business processes, how they sold, the products they represented, how they merchandised them, and most importantly, how they made money—not just gross sales, but profits. I flat-out copied many of the processes, with their blessings. Why copy others instead of doing my own thing? We all know people who have to do things the hard way. Not me if I can help it. Why reinvent the wheel if you don't have to? The processes I emulate are proven winners. Now, not all of them worked for me or in my market, but more often than not, they did. A few of the people I emulated became my trusted mentors, and I listened closely to their advice, warnings, and encouragement.

One word of caution: you can't listen to just anyone. It is not uncommon to meet travel agents at events who may give the impression they are something that they are not. I call them "posers." I remember once when I was still fairly new in the business and happened to strike up a conversation with the man sitting next to me at a cruise event. He was older than me and seemed to be a seasoned agent. I was particularly interested in Crystal Cruises at the time, so I started by asking about his experience with them. He ranted about their reservations department's lack of knowledge, service, and so on (note: I have found most unsuccessful agents tend to have the strongest opinions on any and all subjects). He stated he sold "a lot" of Crystal and they should know who he is and he would never sell them again. Keep in mind that Crystal is, without a doubt, the pinnacle in large-ship luxury cruising and their shore-side staff and service are simply the best. If I owned a luxury cruise line, I would choose Crystal to emulate.

In my inexperience, I thought, "If this guy does a lot of business with them, maybe he is justified in some of his comments." So I asked *the* question: how much Crystal Cruise product do you sell per year? His answer floored me. "About $40,000." Incredulous, I asked him to confirm the number. Keep in mind that $40,000 of Crystal is probably only two or three *staterooms*, and I already selling much more than that.

"That is what the agency sells. I haven't sold any myself—but I want to," he replied. For perspective, an agency that sells "a lot" of Crystal probably books at least $500,000 annually.

Lesson learned—make sure the habits you are emulating are the real deal and not those of a "poser." When you take advice, make sure it's coming from someone who can truly help your business move forward.

The best piece of advice I ever received was also one of the first, and I have lived by it my entire career. When I worked onboard cruise ships in my twenties, I recognized that most of the problems we dealt with onboard tended to be travel-agent related. I saw an opportunity in the travel agency business. It was then that I decided to start a cruise-only travel agency. Back in those days there were probably fewer than 400 cruise specialists in the United States. From the ship where I worked as a purser, I sent letters to five or six cruise-focused and franchise companies for information on starting the business. Not a single one responded—with the exception of Gary Brown, owner of Cruise Shoppes America based in Metairie, Louisiana. Gary explained that they were no longer in the franchise business, but if I was interested, I could join his new consortia and he would help me get up and running. Needless to say, I was interested!

I spent the rest of the year collecting port information, taking tours, and experiencing the destinations as a vacationer. When I departed the Nordic Prince for the final time as a Royal Caribbean employee, I didn't look back. I flew to Miami, loaded up a U-Haul with office equipment, and drove to Metairie.

Gary and I spent three days in his office going through operations manuals and it became very clear to me that I had no idea what I was getting into. I knew I could deliver the service, but running a travel agency—I wasn't so sure. Gary patiently answered even my dumbest questions. At a Cruise Shoppes conference a few months later, Gary hosted the top producers in the organization for dinner and drinks. I wasn't invited. He could see that I felt left out and was jealous of the others. He pulled me aside and said, "Dan, you have to realize these people have invested the time to build their business. It's not fair to compare where you are to where they are today. If you want to get a seat at this table, don't worry about what everyone else is doing. Keep your head down and focus on selling. If you do that, everything else will take care of itself." I took this advice to heart and built a solid company by focusing on the fundamentals of sales.

The key to my success was a series of excellent mentors like Gary. Some I hired, some were customers, and, as I realized later in my career, two of them were my parents. Watching my parents run their own business had a great influence on me, particularly when it comes to risk and how much exposure I am willing to take.

One of my first mentors was Charles "CJ" Johnson who ran the Eagle Snack franchise for Leon Farmer & Company, our local Anheuser-Busch distributor. While I was working on the beer truck and attending school part-time, CJ taught me how to make sales calls and about the importance of building relationships. We focused on the fraternities and sororities at the University of Georgia. We called on eighteen potential accounts and sold seventeen. We were so successful that we were written up in the *Eagle Snacks Times* (an A/B newsletter) and held up as the example for other distributors across the country.

Another mentor, Jim Olson, owned a soap factory and taught me important business practices (and became a good friend). Roy Black, a retired executive, taught me some of the finer points of negotiation as well as the importance of uncompromising integrity and loyalty. There are many others I have acknowledged in the front of this book. Then there were my "competitors" who unselfishly shared their best practices, knowing that it is important that we all succeed. We believe there is more than enough business for all of us. One failure makes the whole travel profession look bad.

I have also worked with hired coaches. A good coach or adviser is worth every penny you invest. Paid advisers have a quality that friends, family, and customers usually don't bring to the table. They typically have firsthand business experience and give you candid feedback without worrying about hurting your feelings or ruining your personal relationship. The feedback I've received from the coaches I've hired has helped me stay focused, stay profitable, and maintain a good work-life balance.

No one succeeds on their own. I owe my success to many and so will you. Carefully choose your mentors and who you will emulate, as they will be a reflection of you and your business.

Inspiration

Let me just start by saying this: I don't believe in motivational speakers. That's not to say that folks such as Tony Robbins are not *inspirational*. While

Tony, Zig Ziglar, Jim Rohn and countless others have inspired millions of people around the world to reach their full potential, their words are just the spark that ignites the fire. Real motivation comes from within.

In high school, I had a friend whose parents were very active in Amway. They had reached the rank of Direct Distributor (pretty good) directly under a Diamond Direct (very good) who lived in our area. As a result, I was exposed to the fruits of building a direct-marketing organization at a relatively young age. This is not a pitch for network marketing businesses, but I have to tell you, it was hard for this poor teenager not to get caught up in it all when I saw how the Diamonds lived. They had a beautiful home, fur coats, custom suits, and of course a Ferrari in the garage. I actually sat in it! Wow! Later, I joined my friend's family in Atlanta at the old Omni Coliseum to hear Amway co-founder Rich DeVos speak. I was mesmerized by his performance, as were the other 20,000 people who filled the arena. He spoke eloquently about how it was our duty to live the American dream. A few days later, I signed up. Then came what Steve Farber, in his book *The Radical L.E.A.P.*, describes as an "OSM" or "oh shit moment"!

Many of you have been in the same situation before—you get caught up in the hype and then when the sponsor moves on to recruit others, you feel like the pumpkin that was once Cinderella's horse-drawn carriage. You feel lost, unfocused, and unsure of where to start or what to do next. How do I know this? I see it in the eyes of thousands of sales professionals at conferences and who attend my workshops every year. Many agents get into the business with good intentions and stars in their eyes, but when it becomes more work than they thought it would be, they are at a loss as to what to do next. They all want to know the secret recipe to success in travel sales.

In the end, I was inspired to join Amway, but I wasn't personally motivated to build that business. It wasn't something that I really wanted to do in my heart. Don't get me wrong, network marketing companies provide wonderful opportunities for those looking for a "business in a box" with minimal investment. I was inspired by what I had seen and heard at the Amway conference, but I was not motivated enough to follow through. Self-motivation is the answer to the question: "Why am I doing this?"

For many sales professionals, the realization of what it really takes to be a successful Wealthy Travel Agent is their wake-up call. Believe it or not, not everyone wants to be the next Warren Buffett or start a company that will disrupt a market and change the world like Facebook. Most people simply want to create a business that will improve their own lives and benefit their friends, family, and community. This is what drives them to follow through on their initial inspiration. But why not dream a little bigger?

You have probably heard the expression that someone has a "burning desire." This "burning desire" is like a fire, and as anyone who has had tenth-grade chemistry can tell you, fire needs three things to burn: oxygen, an ignition source, and fuel.

The fact that you are here reading this is evidence that you process at least one of the key ingredients to make a fire burn—oxygen. It means you are alive, living and breathing. Given the alternative, it's not a bad place to be! It means you have choices and can do anything you want with your life. If you don't like how your life has turned out so far, you can change —it's your choice.

Inspiration is the spark, the ignition source. It's that moment when you realize it is time to actually *do* something you have always want to do. It may be starting a business, making a career change, or going back to school. Each of us has these desires. Some are stronger than others. As I mentioned before, the Tony Robbins of the world inspire us because they help ignite our passion. You probably picked up this book because you've already felt that spark of inspiration to sell travel.

Self-motivation is the fuel source. It's what drives us. It takes the spark of inspiration and turns it into a roaring fire of burning desire. But we have all seen what happens when we leave a fire unattended, when we let it slowly burn out. As long as we keep putting wood on the fire, it will continue to burn indefinitely.

That motivation has to be there for the long run, long after the initial spark of inspiration has faded.

We have already established you have at least two of the three components of a burning desire. You are alive and at some point you were inspired to become a sales professional. But what about the third component? What is the fuel that keeps you going day in, day out? What is your self-motivation?

Motivation comes from a sense of purpose, and successful sales professionals have an overwhelming sense of this. It is the *why* in why we do what we do. Ask yourself these questions:

1. Why did I become a travel sales professional?
2. Is it the same reason today as it when I started?
3. Am I constantly motivated to actively work on my business?

Don't be afraid if your motivation changes. You are just using a different fuel. I originally became a travel salesperson because I recognized an opportunity to provide the same level of service to my customers that they received on their cruise vacation. As my career has progressed, my motivations have changed. Today, the burning desire to help others become sales leaders is what gets me out of bed in the morning. Under it all is my real motivation, the fuel that never runs out. I am still that kid who hates tuna fish, who learned to love the written word, and who is determined to never ever be poor again. This is my fuel, my self-motivation—what's yours?

The clearer you can be in your purpose, the more focused on success you will be. My point is everyone has their own reason, their own purpose, their own motivation that drives their actions. I know what drives me. If you don't know what fuels you, I strongly suggest that you take a step back and figure it out before you do anything else. Remember, the more fuel you add to the fire, the brighter it will burn.

I would like to share a very personal experience that illustrates the power of purpose. A couple of years ago, I had reached what seemed like a low point in my career. I had let circumstances affect my attitude to the point that I was ready to quit. For me, this was a first. I have always been an optimist, but this affected me so much that it would have been very easy to just say *screw it* and walk away. Thankfully, that's not how I'm wired. After much reflection and a swift kick in the ass from my wife, I focused on the *why*—my motivation and how I could contribute more effectively. I collaborated with the organization where I worked to create a position that focused on areas where I really excelled. That re-energized my passion for the work! Moral of the story: if you don't like what you are doing, always remember *why* you are doing it. If you focus on that, you will get the results you desire. If you can't figure out *why,* maybe it's time to move on.

Perhaps you used to feel that burning desire, but it's gone now. That doesn't mean it's gone forever. When we lose the passion to pursue our business, we need to revisit the three "desire" elements: our freedom to choose a new path, our inspiration to choose this career, and our underlying motivation to reach our goals. If you can define these three elements for yourself, your desire will begin to flicker back to life.

Performance and Planning

You've almost got your S.H.I.P. together. You have first-rate skills, disciplined habits, and the best reason for being in the business, so what is standing in the way of top performance? If you're like many people, the biggest obstacle you face is your own fear. It's pointless to make a plan if you are too afraid to execute it. You must face up to and overcome your fears to achieve a high level of performance. Only then can you plan for the future.

The Dan Chappelle you see today was a very different person thirty years ago. Though I grew up on an artist commune, I rebelled against my parents. I wanted to be a clean-cut business person so badly I could taste it. My parents even gave me a trench coat and a Samsonite briefcase one year for Christmas. I was an overconfident people-person, and I believed I could sell anything to anyone.

I came across an ad in the *Red and Black*, the student-run newspaper at the University of Georgia, about a job selling books door-to-door and the riches to be made in just a few short months. Ever the optimist, I signed up right away. This job was the first of many IC roles I have had in my sales career. There were about sixty of us from UGA sent to Nashville, Tennessee, home of the Southwestern Company, along with thousands of other college kids from across the country. We bunked four to a room. We studied all day, memorized our sales talk, role-played, drank a few beers, and slept a little, and then at the end of the week, we received our assignments.

My group from Georgia was going to Washington State, and we were all stoked to be headed out west. I had traveled most of the United States in the back of our van, but I had never been to the Pacific Northwest. Three days, one blown transmission, and two flat tires later, we pulled into Seattle. But we were not quite there yet. A short ferry ride later, we arrived in the sleepy Navy town of Bremerton, Washington, home of the Puget Sound Naval Ship Yard. After we got settled in, we spent the next day "casing" the neighborhoods where we would be selling student handbooks and dictionaries. By the end of the summer, our exploits would fill volumes, but on that first day, I was scared to death.

During our training in Nashville, they told us that it was rare for someone to actually slam the door in your face. At precisely 7:32 a.m., I knocked on my first door and the man who answered took one look at me and *wham*! He slammed the door right in my face before I could even open my mouth to speak. I am willing to bet nothing like this has never happened to you when you've made prospecting calls, has it? At 7:33 a.m., I was done for the day. In fact, to hell with this—I was going home!

I grabbed my sales kit and headed to the closest McDonald's. I wandered around the area for the next two days, contemplating my next move, afraid to even try again. On my Tuesday night check-in call with my sales manager, he sensed all was not well in "DanLand." He said he would come over in the morning to go out selling with me. This was my OSM, I thought. He showed up early the next day and I decided to come clean and tell him what I had not been doing—knocking on doors.

"No worries," he said. "Just follow me for a few hours." And off we went.

First door: nice lady, no thank you. We literally *ran* to the next house, and the next, and the next, until the fifth house invited us in to see the books. They didn't buy—but the next house did. That was a $35 commission that he earned out of *my* territory. I was pissed! But more importantly, I thought, "Wow, it's really that easy." If they said no, it didn't matter, I just went to the next door. Every door was a new opportunity.

I realized the problem was not the prospect on the other side of the door; they had forgotten all about me before the door had even closed. The problem was me, and it was at that moment, I stopped taking rejection personally. To this day it is one of the greatest lessons I have learned in the game of life! I overcame my fear of rejection and so can you. I only had a half dozen or so doors slammed all summer. One of them, I tried an old trick I had heard about in sales school—I ran to the back door and knocked again. I told the lady that I hoped she was much nicer than the one who answered the front door. She started laughing and invited me in. Turned out she was a child psychologist and bought every book I had in my kit.

It is easier to act our way into proper thinking than it is to think our way into proper action. *Action cures fear.* I once had an agent who called me constantly: "I'm losing sales because I don't have my business cards yet, I can't book online, and I don't know how to build an invoice." Blah, blah, blah! He expected everyone to do everything for him instead of taking action himself to build his database and get out to find prospects. Needless to say, his business never got off the ground—because he made excuses instead of taking action.

We all have fears, but the truth is that most of them are perceived and self-sabotaging. Virtually all successful sales professionals have been up against the same issues that you face daily. Talk to mentors, your agency, or your consortia so that you can take the actions needed to build a successful sales funnel.

If you are having troubles, reach out and ask for support. Many resources are there to help you. Nobody can do it for you, but that doesn't mean you can't get a helping hand.

As business owners and salespeople, we have to be in the game every day and yes, some days are harder than others. If we have a strong purpose, healthy attitude, and are willing to take action every day—fear won't impede our performance!

Planning

How will you know the right action to take to "cure" your fear? That's where planning comes in. The typical business spends countless hours planning for the future. They will build out three- to five-year plans, complete with financial and sales projections. Why? Because this is how business planning is taught, and it is the generally accepted way to plot your course. I have always been somewhat skeptical of this process. These plans are based on a number of assumptions that typically far outweigh the facts. Apparently, I am not the only one who feels this way. In their book *REWORK*, Jason Fried and David Heinemeier Hansson take it a step further. They don't bother with the politically correct terms, nope—they call that kind of planning what it really is, a guess.

They have a point. We have been taught to make three-year guesses and five-year guesses. You can plan all you want, but can you predict political situations, economic conditions, changes in spending habits, fads? No, not even the oddsmakers in Las Vegas are that good. Even when future plans are based on past results, it is considered a S.W.A.G.—a scientific wild-ass guess. Scientific or not, it is still a guess.

I am not against planning—in fact quite the opposite. It is essential to have a road map to follow. However, as individuals and small-business people, we need to be able to adapt quickly and often so we can take advantage of opportunities when they arise. I know of small businesses - *really* small sole-proprietors, that have let excellent opportunities slip through their fingers because they haven't budgeted for or "can't justify" the expense. This is less common with larger businesses with employees. Employees don't play with real money—they play with numbers on a spreadsheet. When it is your business, the money is real, but you still need to be able to take advantage of opportunities, provided they make sense when they come along.

The purpose of most traditional business plans is to obtain funding. Unless you need a loan or an investor, this plan will usually end up in binders, sitting in a drawer or on a shelf collecting dust. "Yup, we have a plan, haven't looked at it in years." Think about all the time and effort that goes into putting together a giant S.W.A.G.! Since this is what most businesses are based on, it's no wonder so many fail.

Now let me ask you this: wouldn't you rather focus your energies on things that matter *now* or in the near future? I think you a lready know how I feel about long-term guessing. However, I am a big fan of one-year, one-page plans for small businesses. You can easily set yearly objectives and break them down into quarterly or monthly plans that are concrete, accurate, and achievable. I am not asking you to agree with me. If you want to spend hours and hours of guessing where you will be in three to five years, be my guest. Personally, I will be working on what I can accomplish during the next twelve months because his is something I can control fairly accurately.

A number of business plan models require you to profile your competition in great detail. I don't care about that. I want you to worry about yourself. When you start worrying about them, you waste energy on speculation. I recommend you keep your head down—not in a hole, but down, working on your business instead of comparing it to someone else's. Let them waste the effort worrying about you.

Set goals and objectives

Setting business goals for the year is where the real work begins. In other words, what is the result you are trying to achieve in the next twelve months? This can be a difficult process. The more specific you can be with your objectives, the more likely you are to achieve them. It is very important to "crystallize" your goals. For example, saying that you want to earn six figures is very vague. Do you mean $100,000, or $500,000, or close to a million? If you say, "I will earn $100,000 in commissions from my top three preferred cruise lines by December 31," you clarify the outcome. You have stated the actual amount you want to earn, and—as equally important—you have set a date by which you will do it.

In his book *The Millionaire Mentor,* Greg Reid writes that "a dream written down with a date becomes a goal." What do you want to achieve and by what date? Take a few minutes and think about it. Once you have crystallized your goals, the next step is to write them down. Hang them on your refrigerator, make them your screen saver, write them on a card in your wallet. Look at them every day. Commit them to memory!

Plan your work

Notice that you will not find time management as a topic in this book. I am a firm believer in the Tim Ferris notion of time management and that is to get rid of it.

As a veteran of corporate life, I know there is an expectation that the calendar is always full. Someone I once worked with told me that if it's not in her calendar, it doesn't exist. As a result, her calendar was always booked solid. Her boss might have looked at the calendar and concluded that she was one busy gal who was getting a lot done. Actually, the opposite was true, and the problem lay in the calendar. This person had her workday so tightly planned that if a meeting ran long, which they frequently did, everyone else's schedule was affected by a cancellation or rescheduling. Unfortunately, this paralyzed the decision-making process, and projects were consistently behind schedule.

As an entrepreneur, you don't have the luxury of delaying decisions or getting behind—if you do, you don't eat! I'm not saying get rid of your calendar, but use it as a tool, not a crutch. The secret is not to fill your calendar, but to prioritize what goes in it. You focus on the most important things first and then work your way down the list of priorities.

Imagine you're in my office, looking over my shoulder. Let's open my calendar. My physical and Outlook calendars look the same—fairly empty. You would see appointments and calls, but never more than three or four things per day. Now, look at my desk and you will see a steno pad with a list of things to *accomplish*—not things to *do*. There are typically three to five items on this list. I set my priorities, not based on what's important to other people, but based on what's most important to me and my business.

Make a list of the things you need to accomplish each day to achieve your goals, and put them in order from most to least important. This will keep you focused on the activities that are the most critical. I'll give you a hint where you should start. The only way to grow your business is to create customers. This means prospecting should be a daily priority. In fact, it should be at or near the top of your list every day.

If you have identified your desired end result for the year, how you plan your work will give you the roadmap to get there, much like a sailor plotting a course to the next harbor. For example, in order to achieve the example goal of $100,000 in incremental commissions, you can do some simple math to find out how many cruises you need to sell per day to achieve that goal. Don't divide that goal by 365 days unless you want to work every day of the year! You can think in weekdays (there are 260 of them), weeks, or months. The $100,000 commission goal works out to $8350 per month, $1925 per week, or $385 per day. Assuming you are selling primarily contemporary products, this works out to about one or two sales per working day. If you sell to affluent travelers it might only take two sales per week to hit your goal.

It starts with setting a daily goal based on your need. The next step is determining how you will leverage the tools at your disposal—social media, flyers, e-mail, and telephone, as well as your customer relationship management (CRM) tool—to grow and nurture your prospect database. In my experience, most people don't follow plans that cover a period longer than 90 days. Any more seems out of reach and there is no sense of urgency. However monthly, weekly, and especially daily goals create a strong sense of urgency and are more likely to keep you on track. Need to sell 120 cruises? Overwhelming—you'll work on it later. But sell one or two a day, or five to ten per week, seems pretty achievable and something you can do right now! You're much more likely to tackle that goal with enthusiasm.

Work your plan

This step involves taking action to work the plan you have developed. Similar to sailing a boat or flying a plane, put your trust in the plan—the course you have plotted—and continuously apply the things that work, making adjustments as needed. For example, if your plan was based one or two Carnival or Royal Caribbean sales per day, but the commission on two sales falls below your target, consider changing your product mix to sell higher-priced products like Princess or Holland America (which in most cases would cover your target with a single sale).

It is important that you share your plan and create accountability with someone close to you— someone without a vested interest in your success. Not a business partner, not a spouse, not an employee. You'll review your plan and the progress toward your goals with this objective person. If you don't have someone like this in your life, I strongly suggest that you participate in a monthly private or group coaching call. The investment is minimal, and you will have a professional adviser and a peer group to hold you accountable. They will be open and honest with you. If you need a swift kick in the ass, they will give it to you. If you are not working the plan and doing the activities required to achieve your goals, they will cut you loose. If this sounds harsh, it's not. That's what real accountability looks like.

Know your numbers

It's critical to set daily goals, but do you know exactly how hard you need to work to achieve them? To sell two cruises, do you need to make ten calls a day or fifty? Maybe it'll be easy to hit your targets at first—but what about when you burn through your existing client database and you're only two months in? You can't manage what you can't measure, so it's important to always know your numbers.

When I sold books, my goal each day was to knock on a hundred doors, show the books thirty times, and sell five sets. By tracking these numbers, I was able to predict with a certain amount of accuracy how much I would earn on a daily basis. If you find that for every thirty calls you make, you are able to have ten vacation conversations, prepare quotes for three, and book one, you can track this information and estimate your closure ratio. If you want to sell more, you will need to figure out, based on history, how many more calls, vacation conversations, and quotes are needed to book the desired number of trips.

As a travel agent, you have access to some of the most powerful tools offered by any industry, typically for a nominal fee. These tools may even be a complimentary benefit of your consortia or host agency membership. Most agents use them for invoicing and to manage their CRM—but not to track their prospecting stats. Often the agent is afraid of what the numbers will reveal, so they tend to be ignored. Use the CRM reporting functions to track your sales, commissions, and much more!

Your numbers are more than just sales-related metrics. You also need to keep up with your expenses. The best way to earn more profit is to reduce operating expenses. This means analyzing everything. Start with monthly costs, everything from your utilities to your printer paper. Don't forget technology expenses. Many software programs now offer a monthly subscription model. Microsoft Office 365 is worth the investment and is essential to Windows users. It updates itself and is available across all of your devices. Accounting services such as QuickBooks are also a good investment.

However, subscription services are also the easiest to forget. Don't lose control of your monthly expenses. Make a list of your subscriptions and other monthly expenses: which are indispensable? Which have you completely forgotten about? Which make you money? Which are redundant? Get rid of any expense that isn't critical to your business operation.

MASTERING THE MINDSET

"The reason that so few people are financially independent today is that they place many negative roadblocks in their heads. Becoming wealthy is, in fact, a mind game."
—Dr. Thomas J. Stanley

It's time to really start developing the mindset of the Wealthy Travel Agent. We often hear the expression, especially in sports, that "success is a state of mind." It's true for the travel sales professional as well. Once you start thinking like a WTA, the rest will come relatively easily. As the late Earl Nightingale, author of the legendary program *Lead the Field,* said, "It all starts with attitude."

People will see you for what you are. We each make a conscious choice as to how we are going to face each day. I can wake up and tell myself that this day will be the greatest day of my life, or I can roll over and think about how crappy it will be. I choose the first option. I have a sign on the wall above my desk which reads, "Yesterday is history, tomorrow is your future. Today is your life. Live it!" A good positive attitude toward life and work can influence the outcome of almost any situation. Do people like to be around you or do they go out of their way to avoid you? Think about someone you know who seems to attract others into their circle. People want to be around this person because he or she exudes a positive, confident attitude.

You have probably had people in this business say you can't make any money as a travel agent. Henry Ford said, "Whether you think you can or you think you can't—you are right." If you believe you can't make money selling travel, then you won't, but if you believe you can, you will. Believe me—the opportunity is richer than ever in the history of the travel industry. It's your choice.

A habitually good attitude and belief in yourself are the most important factors in determining your success. If you listen to the naysayers and allow your attitude to reflect their belief, you will never succeed at anything. I believe that, but it is because I made a choice to believe it, and I do my best to keep a positive attitude toward personal life and work life. We have a saying in our house: "Tell me what you can do, not what you can't." If you believe, you can do anything you want. This includes being a successful travel professional with a thriving practice of affluent travelers.

When I first started my company, the Wealthy Travel Agent, the mention of the name drew snickers and criticism from a number of travel "professionals." They didn't believe it was possible to achieve the levels of success I talked about. I am here to tell you—you can, and there are many who are making a very good living in this profession by anyone's standards, simply because they have a great attitude and believe in themselves. Fortunately, the industry is growing and is in desperate need of true professional sales and business people.

Several years before I went to work on cruise ships, I taught SCUBA diving in Athens, Georgia. I often took my students to Panama City, Florida, for their certification dives. We had our choice of many dive operators, but I, like many other instructors from throughout the southeast, used Hydrospace Dive Center. Hydrospace was the largest dive operator in the region, but it wasn't always.

The manager of the operation was a slight young man named Scotty. He was one of those people who made everyone feel special. His infectious, energetic, sometimes over-the-top greeting of "Hey man, how you doing!" and general exuberance made me (and many other dive instructors) want to come back time and time again. Any operator could take us to the same dive sites in the Gulf of Mexico as Hydrospace, but Scotty and his team, who all tried to emulate him, made us feel special. Hydrospace profited for years. Their collective attitude attracted us. We had a choice. So do you. The best thing about it is—it costs nothing to choose a good attitude.

In any type of sales business, there are a number of people who do very well. There are also a large number who have no business being in that business. And then there are those in the middle. These folks haven't quite figured it out and tend to spend more time worrying about things out of their control than those they can control. They have the potential to be great, but they're constantly getting in their own way.

This brings me back to the mindset of the Wealthy Travel Agent. Jokes about the name aside, the WTA mindset is a belief, something to aspire to. We are fortunate to have chosen a business so full of opportunity. In fact, I believe the next twenty years will be the best ever. The tools are evolving and will be different in the future, but the opportunity lives. It is our responsibility to take advantage of it.

Just because others are floundering, lost in the vast sea of opportunity, don't let yourself get caught up in the negativity and mediocrity. Becoming the Wealthy Travel Agent is a choice, and the only person who standing in the way is you. Keep your head down, stay focused on your own plan, and never stop believing in yourself, and you, too, will master the WTA mindset.

Get rid of the C.R.A.P.!

I first heard this expression while watching a TED Talk and fell in love with it! I should have worked at NASA because, as you will read throughout this book, I am a fan of acronyms. (In fact, I have managed to use three acronyms so far in this short paragraph!) C.R.A.P. stands for criticism, rejection, assholes, and pressure—you don't need any of them. This C.R.A.P. will inevitably show itself and threaten to derail your WTA mindset, so be on the lookout.

Criticism

Whenever you are making a change in your life or business, there will always be the naysayers, those who will criticize your every move. These are the people who my kids refer to as KIAs (know-it-alls). They will almost always have something negative to say, especially about how and why you can't do something. They already have all the answers and an opinion about everything. It doesn't matter if you are making a career change or deciding whether to have the apple fritter or the maple bar for breakfast, they always know what's best for you. These are the whiners and complainers. Keep in mind these same people usually have accomplished very little in their own lives.

When you receive criticism, consider the motives of the person offering it. Are they a KIAs without any success of their own? Or are they genuinely trying to help? Just because a criticism is offered doesn't mean you have to take it—even if it's well-intentioned.

Rejection

I addressed this in detail earlier in this section. Rejection is something we all have to deal with in our lives. The key is not to let it affect you personally. If a

prospect says no, it is usually because of a lack of
need or the wrong timing. Very rarely is rejection in
business about you, so don't make it personal. Turn
off that pesky little negative voice in your head and
keep moving forward. Rejection—or, more
accurately, the fear of rejection—can be debilitating.
There is a very old, worn-out, but true saying in sales:
"Each *no* gets you closer to a *yes!*" Don't let fear of
rejection cripple your efforts before you even get
started.

Assholes

My favorite—get rid of them! We all have our
own definition of assholes and you know who they
are in your life or business. If you have managed to let
one into your circle of friends, now is the time to
move on. Chances are, he or she (they come in all
genders) will not even notice. The ones I am talking
about are your prospects and clients. They are the
bullies. These people will sap every ounce of energy
you have, beat you up verbally, and threaten you—
why? Because without them as a customer, you will
fail miserably and it is their duty to remind you of this
as needed. They just can't help themselves—after all,
they are assholes! I have a simple solution. Don't look
at them as a problem. This is an opportunity to clean
house. Let them know that, as a customer, they no
longer fit the way you do business, and you will be
happy to refer them to another travel agency. Bullies

thrive on weakness, so take a stand and they will quickly change their tune and play by your rules, or they will move on to where they can get away with their BS. Either way, you win!

Pressure

Letting go of the pressure is one of the harder things in life. I get it, we all have bills to pay and people to please. In the big scheme of things, few people really care about what we have going on in our lives, and most of the pressure we feel is self-imposed. The key is to recognize real pressure, such as a hard deadline to get a quote to a prospect, versus pressure we create ourselves, like making a promise that is hard (or impossible) to deliver. Once we distinguish between the two types of pressure, we can prioritize them—and avoid adding additional, created pressures to our lives. It's also important to find our own release valve. The Seattle area where I live is known for its beautiful outdoor recreation opportunities, and hiking is my outlet. It is just me and the trail, with an occasional elk or bear to keep me on my toes. It is here where I sort out the real and perceived stresses of my week. The result is both physically and mentally exhilarating.

Overcome fear and intimidation

"One of the greatest discoveries a man makes, one of his greatest surprises, is to find he can do what he was afraid he couldn't do."
—Henry Ford

The biggest battle that we all face isn't with our competitors. It's the conflict we face within ourselves, and the quicker that we learn to master the mindset of the Wealthy Travel Agent, the faster we'll be on the path to our objectives.

Any time we deal with people who we perceive to have wealth, fame, or power, there's a certain amount of intimidation. How we deal with this intimidation is important. The first thing to remember is this: you are the problem. That's right! If you want to do business with important people, you will need to overcome your perceptions. To them, you are a problem solver. After all, why should they consider doing business with you unless you're solving a problem for them? So start thinking that way.

It's important to remember that the wealthy and powerful are people just like you and me. They eat, sleep, and drink like us, even if they are very different in terms of education, income, and lifestyle. They aren't any better than us, even though it might feel that way. For many of us, thinking of ourselves as inferior started when we were kids. We desperately wanted the approval of our parents and teachers, and maybe we didn't always get it. We wanted to sit next to the pretty girl or the cute boy on the bus but were afraid he or she would laugh at us. We started early believing we weren't good enough or good-looking enough for people whose opinions we valued.

As we grow older, the fear of rejection, of *not making it*, becomes more real. The tryouts for the school sports team. College admissions. Our first "real" job interview. A marriage proposal. It's no wonder that people develop a fear of rejection and focus on the negatives. There's a lot at stake! If you have dealt with the fear of rejection most of your life, how do you get over it? It really boils down to facing up to our fears and acting in spite of them. Remember this phrase: *"Action cures fear."*

Do you tend to worry about things that "might" happen to you? Do you run through different scenarios and outcomes in your mind over and over until you are scared shitless? This is natural, since as human beings we are conditioned to focus on the negative in most situations. The truth is if we just took action and faced up to those fears, we'd find that really there's not much to them. We must have confidence that we can overcome our fears.

Develop confidence

One thing I've learned in a lifetime of sales and business is how large a role self-confidence plays in achieving success. I'm not talking about false confidence or pretending to be something you aren't. I'm talking about real confidence that comes from knowing that you have something valuable to contribute to a transaction or relationship. Real confidence builds trust with your clients. One of the easiest ways to gain self-confidence and the trust of your clients is by developing expert-level knowledge of the product you are selling.

A few months after I opened my first travel company, a woman came in and said she wanted to go to the Four Seasons on the island of Nevis. I had been to nearby St. Kitts many times while working on cruise ships, but never Nevis, though I'd read the name on maps. I had never heard it pronounced aloud, so I corrected her. "It's pronounced 'Nevis,' not 'Neevis.'" After all, I was the Caribbean expert. With what must have been monumental patience, she told me she had been there several times and it *is* pronounced "Neevis." Needless to say, I never saw her again and have since learned the correct pronunciation.

My false confidence ruined the transaction. This is a classic rookie mistake, and customers can see it from a mile away. Have you ever gone to a car dealer and a young salesperson spots you from across the lot? He's got the pursuit angles he learned playing high school football down pat, ready to intercept you as you walk by.

He catches up with you and greets you, so you ask a question about a particular vehicle. It quickly becomes clear that he doesn't know what he's talking about. He hasn't taken the time to learn about the products he sells. He is not familiar with the vehicle other than it has four wheels. He has no idea about gas mileage or other system features and benefits of that particular model. He's trying, but he either spouts nonsense or has to refer to the brochure or check with his manager about everything. As a consumer you don't trust in his abilities. You will not purchase anything today—from him.

However, another salesperson comes around as you're wandering the lot, and she starts asking you questions about your driving habits, your needs for the vehicle, and what features are important to you. In general, this salesperson appears to be very knowledgeable about the products she is selling. Needless to say, you feel more comfortable with the second salesperson than the first. Confidence is key. It helps make everyone relax, and as a result, the sales process is less stressful. If the salesperson is confident in her product knowledge, the customers are confident that the salesperson is going serve their best interest. They feel good about what they're buying. And they'll be loyal to her! Even if their next vehicle is a different make, they will refer their family and friends back to her.

Don't worry about the competition

I don't want you to get caught up in worrying about what the other guys are doing. You've heard that voice in the back of your head (or maybe you've heard it from a colleague): "You know, XYZ travel agency is selling this cruise for this amount of money and we're selling it for that amount of money. We need to drop our prices to be competitive!" The reality is that if most agents would spend as much time thinking about their own business, and working on their own business, as they do about everybody else's, they would be much more successful. Stay focused on your goals and objectives. It's fine to be cognizant of what the competition is doing, but don't become obsessed about it. Let them worry about you, not the other way around. You know what you need to do to be profitable. Don't undercut your success by sabotaging your plans in an attempt to match another agent's business model.

Commit to a standard of excellence

What is it that you want to be known for? Hopefully, you want to be known for a high level of integrity, honesty, and fairness. Commit to a standard of excellence that you will provide to your customers and your suppliers. I'm often quoted as saying, "Everyone wins." That's my objective—not for me to win and you to lose, but for all of us to win. There's enough business out there for everyone, whether you're in the travel agency, real estate, or insurance business. We don't need to elbow each other out of the way on price to get customers. Instead, we each need to focus on finding new talent and new prospects.

As a travel agent, I often referred prospects to other travel agencies if their requests were outside my area of expertise. The customers appreciated this practice, and when they had a need for my particular area of expertise, they sought me out again. I didn't lose their loyalty by referring them—I gained it! This may seem counterintuitive, but if you take this approach, customers are having conversations with their friends and family and giving out *your* name, not just the name of the agency where you referred them. It's pretty likely that you'll get referrals back from the other agency, too. This kind of generosity, the generosity of referrals, is part of becoming a Wealthy Travel Agent. Sharing the wealth means everyone wins. No one gets to a place of accomplishment on their own. We all have help, and there's enough business out there for all of us to share and still profit.

Understand your relationship with money

Many of us are insecure about one thing or another. For some it is intelligence, and for others it is their appearance. For many of us Wealthy Travel

Agents, a primary insecurity is (or was) how we feel about money.

Before we can lay the foundation for a successful business, we must first address the real and often deep-rooted relationship we have with money. What does it mean to you? How do you define wealth? Webster's Dictionary defines wealth as "a large amount of money and possessions," and for most, wealth is an accumulation of money and things. A large home, exotic sports cars and SUVs in the driveway, designer clothes, household help, luxury vacations, and the list goes on.

How we feel about wealth and money can be traced back to our childhoods. I grew up in a very poor home on an artists' commune. Our living room furniture consisted of an old couch our neighbors had thrown out and a pleather lounge chair with no legs from a local thrift store. Our tables were empty wire spools of different sizes. We had a small black and white TV, which, when it broke, my parents refused to repair because they claimed we were not reading enough. The truth was that they couldn't afford to get it fixed. And let's just say that we didn't eat tuna casserole for Thanksgiving dinner because we didn't like turkey. All we could afford at the time were cans of tuna, cream of mushroom soup, and egg noodles.

Like most kids, I didn't realize how poor we really were—until we visited our aunt and uncle for Christmas one year. Their home was very modern and comfortable, with the 1970s décor that is very much back in style now. What I remember most was they had a bar and central heat (we had a wood stove). *This* was how I wanted to live when I grew up.

At an early age, I rebelled against my hippie upbringing and started wearing what all my friends were wearing—khakis & button downs (although mine were from the thrift store). I wanted what my friends had. What I considered luxuries were normal to them.

Eventually, my parents' pottery business ended up doing very well and roast turkey even made it onto the holiday menu. But the die had been cast. I didn't want to be poor when I grew up, and to this day I will not eat canned tuna. The fear of poverty drives me to succeed. I saw the things my friends and cousins had, compared their lifestyle to mine, and, I admit, I was extremely jealous. Seeing the things money could buy made me feel good. This was something that I wanted. Funny thing, though—they will tell you that they wanted to be me as much as I wanted to be them.

Think about your own relationship with money. Did having it or the lack of it cause pain or jealousy in your life? Did a family member have a drug or alcohol problem that caused every penny your family had to be spent at the liquor store, drug dealer, or failed rehab efforts? The cause of most family splits is not infidelity, it's finances. As such, many people, especially children of divorce, have negative feelings about it. They may engage in wishful thinking: if they had enough money, all their problems would be solved. As the growing list of bankrupt lottery "winners" attests, this is not true.

Do you feel good about money because of the abundance it has provided you? A nice home, cars, boats, and other material things? Or luxuries that are not so obvious, like the ability to get a good education or support the charity of your choice?

It is not uncommon for people to equate their self-worth with the amount of money they make or their job title. I am going to tell you, right here and right now—get over it. Money or job titles do not define your worth as a person.

Your perceptions about money will greatly affect your ability to sell just about anything, including yourself. I don't care if you're selling a car, a cruise, a home, or software—how you feel about money is important because the negative associations you hold can be self-sabotaging. Many salespeople think of buying power in terms of their own income or credit card limits. They're embarrassed or uncomfortable when they sell something that they can't afford themselves. This is an unfortunate, but common ailment. The good news is, it can be cured.

We talk about this all the time in the sales business. It's called "selling out of your own pocket." Let's assume your goal is to regularly sell five- and six-figure vacation packages. Unless you are another Bill Gates, Warren Buffett, or Philip Anschutz, this is not something that, as a salesperson, you can afford to purchase yourself, so you must remove the mental barrier and stop viewing money as something another person has and you don't. Think like most wealthy travelers do: for them, money is a tool to get something they want. Money is not something to fear—it puts the world at their fingertips.

We must see the world as full of endless possibilities. We read about the billionaire tech fortunes in the *Wall Street Journal* every day and can't help but wonder *why not me?* Well, why not you? There were thousands of people making a very good living selling travel in the past, and there will be even more in the future. Who are these Wealthy Travel Agents? They're the agents who are not afraid to work hard and see money for what it is—a tool to help them reach their goals.

I have sold many high five- and six-figure vacations in my career, but I am not going to lie, my butt puckered the first time I made a sale over $100,000. I was sitting at my desk when the phone rang, and the caller explained that he had just got a brochure in the mail from my agency for a trip, and he wanted to book it.

"It's a two-and-a-half week trip by a company called Intrav. It's an 'Around the World' trip on the Concorde."

Sweat was pouring from my forehead. "Right," I said and put him on hold to grab the brochure. I came back on the line and said, "OK, the trip is… $52,500 per person." He said he knew that and wanted to book it. So I took down his information. He was in the database from a list I had purchased, but I had no idea who he was. While I was talking to him, I was also reading the terms and conditions for the trip. Non-refundable, cash or check only. Sweat continued to pour off me. I looked like I had just successfully completed the "Ice-Bucket Challenge" that was so popular a couple of years ago. I swallowed hard and told him the terms.

"Yeah, no problem. I will send my assistant over with a check in the morning. What time do you open?"

Hell, I would have spent the night if he had asked, but I managed to say, "I'll be here at 10 a.m."

After the usual pleasantries and goodbyes, I tried to play it cool, but I couldn't help it. I cut loose with a semi-pornographic happy dance and then poured myself a nice glass of scotch from a bottle I had recently received as a gift from a happy customer. The next morning, right on time, his assistant showed up with the check. By now I was feeling pretty good about myself—after all, it was over $12,000 commission. Did I sit on the check for the next deposit? No. Did I rush to the bank and deposit it? Hell, no! I did what any good business person would do—I called his bank to make sure it was good.

The teller said to me, "Mr. Chappelle, any check from Mr. X will be honored by this bank." Holy crap, who was this guy? Turns out he did have a story. He and his wife were two of the nicest people I ever met, and we did business together for several years until his trips became so complicated that I needed to refer him to someone else. The agent I referred him to always paid me a nice residual. Everyone wins! One more thing, the brochure he received from me was sent through my consortia. They ran my database against their own demographic data. That targeted brochure was one of only three sent on behalf of my agency, so be sure to participate in your host or consortia marketing programs.

CALL TO ACTION

As sales professionals, we are what the IRS refers to as the "1099 workforce." We are the real estate agents, travel professionals, consultants, and salespeople from many different industries. The one thing we all have in common is that we earn our income strictly from commissions and fees. Our income has its ups and downs like any field. However, our livelihood is very different than our salary-based counterparts. As primal as it sounds, it's true: if we don't sell, we don't eat!

Sales as a profession is much like the sea that has been so good to me over the years. We all know there are the crests of the wave, the high points after making a big sale or nailing a presentation. But there are also the troughs, or as I like to call them, "the pits of despair," when it seems no matter what we do, sales just aren't happening. It's how we prepare for the choppy seas that determines how we ride those waves. We all prefer to be riding high on the wave, but inevitably we all find ourselves in the trough of the wave once in a while! Just being cognizant of the ups and downs, we are able to plan for the financial risks and, often more importantly, the psychological effects of this natural cycle of business. The goal is to ride the wave as smoothly as possible, not to end up underwater!

My question to you—is your S.H.I.P. seaworthy? Do you have the skills, habits, inspiration, and performance to carry you through the ups and downs of the sales business? Ask yourself these questions:

1. *Do I have the necessary skills to excel in sales?* The first thing we do when we are in a slump is question our own abilities. Management guru Peter Drucker defines the purpose of a business like ours "to simply create and keep customers." Do you have the prospecting and sales skills to create customers for your company? Are you willing to hire a business adviser or sales mentor to help you develop or grow the skills you need? Are you willing to invest in your professional education to acquire the knowledge needed to be considered an expert in your field? Having confidence in your knowledge and skills is essential to getting through the tough times and can keep you at the top of your field!

2. *"Do my daily habits contribute to or get in the way of my success?"* Our primal motivators are fear versus reward, or pain versus pleasure. These motivators influence our daily habits. For example, if you view calling prospects as a negative, as a potential rejection, then prospecting will cause you fear and pain and you will avoid the habit. However, if you frame those prospecting calls as potential sales, the calls will become a habit that brings you pleasure and reward. The key is to form personal and professional daily habits that contribute to the success of your business.

3. *Why?* This is the most important question. What choices have you made to get here, and what inspired you to enter this field? What gets you out of bed each day and feeds the drive to build your business? If you can't answer this, you need to step back and figure it out. An overwhelming sense of purpose—the "why"—is the most important factor to your success.

4. *Do you have the ability to motivate and manage yourself?* Do you have a plan with short- and long-term goals for your business? Do you plan your day with these goals in mind? Do you hold yourself accountable and seek objective feedback from mentors and coaches? There is a saying that "you can't

manage what you can't measure." Do you understand and use important metrics to measure the health of your business?

If you've answered these questions honestly and completely, your S.H.I.P. is ready to sail!

Chapter 3
The "Business" of the Travel Business

In the travel business, why is one agent or agency considered to be a better choice over another? I believe it boils down to two things, skills and specialty. The objective of this section is to help you find them. Skills and specialty can both be learned, but it will take an investment of time and money to develop them to a level that makes you the obvious choice among consumers.

> *"Formal education will make you a living; self-education will make you a fortune."*
> —Jim Rohn

In any profession there is a certain skill set required to do the job. A tax accountant will not have the same skills as an auto mechanic, and a math teacher will have different skills than an airline pilot. Yet each has the opportunity to excel in their respective roles. Take them out of their natural environment and you may have a disaster. Force them to generalize within their field and they may lose what makes them great.

To see where the concept of specialization has been most successful, we need to look no further than the medical profession. All medical doctors have a foundation education. In medical school they teach the basics, the general medical knowledge and fundamental skills needed for the job. As part of their education, they then intern at a teaching hospital where they put the skills they learned into practice under supervision of a team of experienced physicians.

When they finish their apprenticeship, some may choose to be general practitioners (GPs). A GP is similar to the typical travel professional. They know a little bit about a lot of things. But many will declare a specialty, one that is of interest to them personally and professionally, one that will provide the financial rewards needed to pay off the half million dollars invested in their education.

Over the next few years, doctors will learn to master the skills of that specialty. Cardiologists work on and study the cardiovascular system, dermatologists study the skin, and so on. Physicians choose to specialize partly because it is very difficult to become an expert in many areas, but fairly easy (relatively speaking) to be an expert in one particular field, or even a subset of a field. Surgery is a specialty, but most surgeons take it even further, sometimes even down to a particular extremity or organ of the body. There is a surgeon in the Atlanta area whose practice is exclusively hand surgery, and more specifically carpal tunnel syndrome. Needless to say, he is considered the world's leading hand surgeon. It's all he does and subsequently, his fees are far higher than a general surgeon's. Why? Because people will pay a premium for expert attention and knowledge.

The days of handing a prospect a travel brochure are long over. With the resources available on the internet, your prospects will have spent hours researching every possible detail of their trip. They're not experts, but they know enough to be dangerous. Unless you are a specialist in the type of travel that interests them, you won't bring value to the transaction.

Travel + Leisure, Condé Nast, Wendy Perrin, and others regularly publish lists of the "World's Best" hotels, airlines, tour operators, and travel professionals. Next time you read one of these lists, take notice. They don't say "World's Best Travel Agent" or even "World's Best Luxury Travel Agent." Travel agents can't be the "world's best" for all customers. The lists target specialties like "World's Best Travel Agent, African Safari." The value to the customer is in the specificity. A person who wants to take a safari won't get "world's best" service from an agent who mostly books family cruises, even if the agent is completely competent.

These "world's best" lists are lists of fifty or so of the top specialists in each area. Even though the media sources are competitors, they often have many of the same agents on their lists. Why? Because there are so few travel professionals who truly excel in their area of specialization.

Much like your purpose, your specialty should reflect your passion. For example, if exploring the great cities of Europe is a passion of yours, consider specializing in European River Cruising. If you love to bike, specialize in biking tours—these are extremely popular in parts of the US and across Europe. Whatever you choose as your specialty, this will become the main focus of your business. People ask me all of the time why I chose to mentor travel agents for a living. Simply put, my passion is helping people become as successful as they want to be. I learned this from my own coaches and mentors who felt the same way.

GAINING EXPERTISE

In order to be considered a specialist, it goes without saying that you need to become an expert in the area. This will tremendously increase your value to your customer, and in turn it will increase the commission and fee revenues you will generate.

Customers who seek out a specialist expect to pay more.

Let's say you are a golfer, and you want to buy a new set of clubs. You see a set on sale at Costco for $500. Pretty good deal, right? Well, yes and no. It's a great price and Costco will sell a lot of clubs—but are they the right clubs for your game? In other words, do those clubs solve your problem? A better solution: make an appointment at Golftec or Golfsmith and have a professional analyze your swing and custom-fit the clubs to you. The golf pro will take measurements for shaft length and determine how flexible they should be for your game. You will pay a little more upfront, but for golfers who are serious about their game, they see the real value in this service. The money and time saved from losing balls and chasing after slices or hooks—not to mention an improved handicap and bragging rights—makes it worth every penny. Your customers really don't want to buy the cheapest item; they want to buy goods or services that solve their problem most efficiently.

There are many strategies to master a specialty. Basically, it takes practice. You can get this practice in your everyday work, but experts at the top of their game do more than that. NBA players don't rely on their games to learn all their skills. No, they work their asses off every day in practice. They don't experiment on the court—they run plays and make shots they've tried out dozens or even hundreds of times before during practice. The following strategy is an easy way to gain expertise and develop specialized knowledge. It's certainly not the only way, but this is a type of practice strategy that has helped me. It can help you, too! Even if it's not your usual method, give it a try.

I'll use European river cruises as the example specialty. To become an expert, we need to learn the core river systems and the main destinations on each itinerary. Then we will identify one to three products (brands) and study their ships, staterooms, amenities, style, service, food, excursions, and so on. Try to get to know every nuance about the products. In addition to firsthand experience, YouTube is a great resource.

I'm a visual guy so here is a trick I developed when working on ships to learn new itineraries when assigned to a new ship. I have used it ever since to learn complex regions serviced by a number of suppliers. Picture a coat rack on your wall with six pegs to hold your jackets. Each peg is going to represent a European river. Assign one peg to the Danube, one to the Rhine, and so on. Now, below each peg, list the main embarkation city in bold, followed by the main stops, and end with the disembarkation city. I find it easiest to list north to south or west to east. Just remember what goes up usually goes down—meaning the itinerary may reverse.

Now below each point in the itinerary, list the vessels currently scheduled for that itinerary. At this point, don't worry about what the cruises are called (for example, "Scenic Sounds of the Danube"), just know the cruise is Nuremberg to Budapest. Also, don't worry about which cruise line. The names of the vessels will usually give away the brand (Ama, Viking, and so on).

You may be asking, "Why do I need to learn the itineraries? Shouldn't I focus on the cruise line?" It is important to remember that, whether it's Alaska, the Mediterranean, the Caribbean, or rivers, the main ports don't move or change. The same is true for land tours. The itineraries are basically the same for all brands. However, the hardware can be reassigned based on demand, just like an airplane route. For example, in the summer months Delta may use their larger 767 or 757 aircraft from Seattle to Anchorage. However, in the winter months, they will use the smaller 737 because demand is much lower. The same is true with cruise ships and tour buses. Seasonal demand will determine which ship is assigned to an itinerary.

Don't get hung up on my example (coat hook pun intended). It's not just for European river cruises! You can use the coat hook visual for all cruise and tour regions.

The next area we need to master is knowledge of the region surrounding the itineraries. Your clients want to hire a specialist who has experienced the area and can suggest things to do, or places to visit, that aren't on the usual list of excursions. Nobody wants a cookie-cutter vacation! There are a number of ways to gain this knowledge. First and foremost—spend some time in the region. Nothing beats firsthand knowledge of a destination to boost your confidence. This means you will need to invest in what I call your "professional education." Just like you have invested in this book to improve your skills, you must invest in the travel experience. If a familiarization (FAM) trip is available, take advantage of the opportunity. This is very important—you will want to experience the trip the way your customers will. In addition, there are great resources for learning about a region online, in print, and on TV. Just like itineraries, landmarks and local customs rarely change.

My personal favorite resource for regional research is YouTube. Not only will you get suppliers' promotional videos, but also television shows which have profiled the region, travelers posting their homemade movies—and this is just the start. I was hired to give a thirty-minute presentation to a group of travel professionals about Dubai. Bear in mind, I had never been to Dubai and knew virtually nothing about the destination. So I turned to YouTube for help. I learned more about the region: the city, how the skyscrapers are built, where the water comes from, its striking similarity to the city of Chicago, and more. Needless to say, my audience was blown away! When I visited Dubai a month later, I had a greater appreciation based on my research of the area.

For getting to know European destinations, one of my favorite TV shows is *Rick Steve's Europe Through the Back Door* on **PBS**. This show is a great way to see a region or city through the eyes of a man who has spent a lifetime exploring Europe. I have personally toured and recommended many of the sights, activities, and cafés that I learned about on his shows.

Finally, we will learn about the different brands. This book is not intended to teach product; however, once you learn itineraries and regions, you need to select the type of brand experience you will specialize in selling to your clients. You are selling experiences. Remember the old saying to "sell the sizzle, not the steak"? The sizzle is the experience and the product—the steak—is what delivers the experience. A Tauck experience is very different than an Avalon, and Viking River Cruises is different than Uniworld. They may sail exactly the same itinerary, but the experience will be very different. A good comparison is the experience you have at the Ritz Carlton hotel that is only a block away from a Marriott. Both are owned by the same parent company, but they offer distinct experiences, and the type of experience is usually reflected in the price point.

Using the Danube as our example, Uniworld will consistently deliver what is arguably considered the most upscale experience of all the river cruise products: the suites are spacious and well-appointed, and the food is world class. This would be a good fit for a customer who typically vacations in luxury resorts. Viking is a great product, as well, but offers a deluxe experience. You will have customers for both types of products.

Even within the river cruise segment, you can't be all things to all people. There are over twenty brands (and growing) cruising the rivers of Europe. As a specialist, you will need to focus on two or three brands. There are several reasons for this. Consolidating your sales gives you more power with that brand. You have the ability to earn higher commissions, increased co-op, and possible volume incentives. Not to mention that you can be the go-to agent when they need to move inventory because you will have proven your sales ability!

CHOOSING PARTNERSHIPS

We have all heard the expression "dance with one who brought you." This is a great position if you were the one invited, but in business it is up to you to choose your partners. You have to do the asking, so don't put it off, and choose wisely.

It's your business, so be prudent about who you ask to the dance. Very few people become successful all by themselves. They have a team of hosts, suppliers, and customers all working together to help reach their collective goals. The most important choice you will make as an independent business person is whether or not to work with a consortia and/or host agency. I have heard arguments for both sides, but in my opinion, partnering with a consortia or host agency is the winner—hands down.

On your own, you will receive the full commission for your sales, most likely at the base level of 10 percent. However, you will need to produce your own marketing materials and negotiate your own supplier contracts—not to mention develop and maintain your own website. The list of hats you'll have to wear goes on and on, and at some point you will need to find some time to sell something! Maybe that's what you signed up for when you became a travel professional, but my guess is—if you wanted a job, you would just go out and get one. When you are on your own, you are just that, on your own.

So how do you choose a consortia or host agency? Consortia and host agencies typically offer many of the same services. The host agency of today is what the consortia started as in the 1980s. They were commission clubs. An agency would join and all the sales revenue was rolled up into one large pool. As a result, most suppliers paid the members of these organizations commissions at their highest compensation levels of 15 percent or more. As many of the suppliers (especially cruise lines) became public companies, shareholder pressure to control distribution costs led them to institute a tiered-commission schedule like you see today. Today, the role of the consortia/franchisor has shifted from a commission club to marketing organizations supporting your sales efforts.

The travel industry has more business models than you could ever imagine. The tiered commissions made it impossible for the "little guy" to compete with the national agencies, particularly those with a price-driven model that rebated a portion of the commission in order to have the lowest price. As a result, the host agency model was created. By bringing independent agencies and agents under the host agency umbrella, everyone wins. The supplier gets an agency (the host) focused on consistently achieving the top sale tiers. You (the agent) receive a higher commission than if you were on your own, and the host agency takes a cut of the commissions. Most host agencies, regardless of size, are usually part of a consortia to take advantage of additional marketing resources, technology, and supplier relationships.

As a member of a host agency, your company will have resources at its disposal that would cost hundreds of thousands of dollars to create and maintain on your own. Yes, it's true that the host will receive a portion of the commission in exchange for the services offered by it and the consortia, but in the end you will still come out ahead. There really is "strength in numbers."

Let's look at my other favorite business model for validation. A real estate agent is affiliated with a brokerage firm. That brokerage firm provides brand and marketing resources as well as several commission-split and fee options. The broker is a host agency for a number of real estate agents. Some brokers provide leads to agents, while others offer minimal support based on the agent's needs. The same basic model is used in travel.

Host agencies come in many shapes and sizes, with a variety of options. Some are franchised brands such as Travel Leaders, Expedia CruiseShipCenters, CruiseOne, and Cruise Planner. Others are agencies such as Travel Experts, Avoya, Travel Society, Nexion, and Montrose that are members of consortia such as Virtuoso Signature, Travel Leaders Group (formally Vacation.com), or Ensemble. This is by no means an exhaustive list.

The options are many, so it is important take a hard look at your business model and understand what *your* business needs before pulling the trigger on membership. A couple of good resources are Travelliance's *Black Book of Host Agencies,* the Professional Association of Travel Hosts (PATH), and The Travel Institute. Some are hosts are full service, cruise and tour only, or luxury focused. Others allow you to benefit from marquee brands such as American Express, Travel Leaders, and Expedia.

Some key benefits to look for from a host agency include the following:

- Personalized Website
- E-mail marketing
- Integrated CRM
- Systems training

- Supplier relationships
- Visibility to suppliers
- Seller of Travel (SOT) licenses
- Insurance programs and certifications

You should also inquire about any monthly fees for technology or marketing, the commission splits, and franchise fees. Remember, the relationship has to work for both parties—this is one of the most important decisions of your business. View the fees and commission splits as an investment, just like your professional education and other business-related expenses.

Suppliers

Your host or consortia is probably preferred with all of the major vendors with either a fixed- or tiered-commission scale. This needs to be taken into consideration when you are forecasting sales and cash flow. Assuming your model is one where your primary vendors fall into the deluxe, luxury, and specialty segments, choose your consortia or host based on their relationships with these vendors. The most important questions to ask is "Are they easy to do business with?" or ETDBW. What does that mean to you? It means they have automated booking, accurate commission calculations, timely commissions payment (also known as cash flow!), co-op funding, local representation, and quick resolutions to any issues or discrepancies. If you are not familiar with these practices, talk to your host or consortia. They will be happy to assist.

Specialization is important for your working relationships. You can only become an expert with a limited number of suppliers—in fact, the fewer the better. More importantly, the supplier will see your focus on their product and usually provide additional resources over and above those received via host relationship in recognition of your efforts. In the end, it's about money. If you are spreading your business around, a little here and a little there, you will never build the volume needed to get on the radar of the local or national representatives. If you are focused and submit a realistic sales plan, many vendors will give you an upfront commission increase and co-op for a limited time to help kick-start your efforts.

Local representatives, or business development managers (BDMs) as they are also known, typically have large geographic territories. They receive a substantial amount of their compensation based on hitting production targets in their region. As a result, they are stretched for time and resources, so they will focus on proven agents who produce substantial revenue. Depending on the supplier, substantial could mean as little as $50,000 or as much as $1 million or more.

If you want to get a BDM's attention, request a meeting and ask this one simple question: "What can I do to help you achieve your goals for the territory?"

Make sure you are very clear that this meeting will be a valuable use of their time. Everyone always wants something from them, usually more commission or co-op, but very few view the relationship as a partnership. Partners support each other, so have clear, realistic objectives as part of the plan you present. In my experience, many agents have a false sense of entitlement and believe that the supplier owes them something. In fact, they don't owe any of us anything.

If you are new or just beginning to specialize in a product or destination, your sales plan will be the key to opening the door to a call or meeting with the BDM. Make sure you have a clear purpose for the meeting and a desired outcome. This can be communicated in advance with an agenda. Be respectful of his or her time and stick to the agenda so the BDM knows what to expect. Most BDMs will be blown away by your organization and professionalism.

You need to have some skin in the game. Make sure you are prepared to pay at least 50 percent of the cost for any advertising or event you propose. Let's face it, if you are not willing to invest in your own idea, what makes you think the supplier would do so? Treat the partnership for what it is and don't take unfair advantage of the BDM's time or money.

If you have an idea that you think will revolutionize travel in your area, such a partnering with a local chef for a haggis-tasting journey of

Scotland, and the BDM politely suggests there may be better ways to spend your collective efforts—you might want to listen. Odds are, they have seen and tried it ninety-nine times with little success, so it's doubtful that the hundredth time will be a winner. If you work from home, plan on meeting for coffee or lunch. Don't expect them to come to your house. Remember, you are not only representing yourself, but also your consortia, agency, and host agency. It's important to maintain a professional image that others can look up to and aspire to emulate.

Lastly, if you really want to make a strong, lasting, professional impression, buy your BDM lunch or coffee. This small gesture sends the signal you are serious, professional, and have the partnership approach. Your relationship will stand a much better chance of succeeding if you get to know them on a personal level. Don't just keep the conversations about business. Ask appropriate questions about their family, hobbies, and interests outside of work. You should be prepared to answer the same questions. Remember, people do business with people they like—so let them like you.

Often in the sales profession, we end up working for several different companies throughout our career. It is no different for BDMs. It is not unusual for a BDM to represent two to four different companies in their career. I know of one who intentionally changes employers every few years. BDMs rely on the relationships they have built with

www.DANCHAPPELLE.com

travel agents over the years to sell the product they are representing at the time.

The lesson here is that we tend to be loyal to people, not brands. If your BDM for brand A moves to brand B, you will have the advantage of an established working relationship with the BDM and not have to start from scratch with their new product—one you may or may not already be selling. This is one of the many reasons you should treat your BDM like family. You never know where they may end up.

It is crucial to operate from a place of uncompromising integrity. You have a business relationship with your suppliers, and your actions speak volumes. Treat suppliers' representatives, BDMs, reservation agents, inside sales support, and even the president of the company the way you want to be treated as a human being. It is unprofessional to bully, threaten, yell, lie, or curse at the person on the other end of the phone. While you may not always agree with someone, don't take anything personally. Both parties have the same objective, so yelling at a reservation agent or threatening to "off sell" one brand to another not only makes you look bad, it isn't going to win you any friends. As large as the travel industry seems, it is actually a fairly small community of professionals, and you want to make sure you have friends who can help when you really need it.

In my role as a cruise-line sales executive, I gave very specific instructions to the head of our reservations team. If a travel agent was rude or disrespectful to them, he was instructed to bring it to my attention if he felt it was warranted. Res agents have pretty thick skin, but when a travel agent displays inappropriate behavior, we would take immediate action. First, we would listen to the recording—yes, all conversations are recorded. Depending on the severity of the negative interaction, we would either send a quick e-mail to the agent, reach out to the agency and/or consortia management to discuss, or, in extreme cases, decline to do business with the agent in the future. As a professional, always treat everyone with respect. Be the agent others look up to and aspire to emulate.

Don't be the Shrimp Lady

FAM trips are a great way to learn about experiences and destinations. However, if they not available, you should be willing to invest the full price of the vacation in order to experience it in the same manner as your guests. You will be a much better salesperson for it.

FAMs are designed to be fun, learning experiences and the vast majority of agents behave in a respectable and professional manner. However, there are always a few who give the profession a black eye. I have seen a number of travel agents over the years treat FAMs as their own personal holiday at the supplier's expense. Unfortunately, this behavior is more common than one might think and as a result, most suppliers are now more selective with their invitations.

Suppliers invest substantial resources in these programs. The biggest sign of disrespect is to be a no-show for meetings and events. They don't do these for their health. The events are an opportunity for you to get to know the management and staff as well as your peers. If you don't attend the meetings, it's likely you won't be invited back.

Also, just because the food and booze are free, that doesn't make it OK to overindulge in either. I have personally witnessed an agent dumping a bowl of shrimp into her handbag while others reach behind the bar to grab bottles of liquor to take back to their rooms. One word—unacceptable. If you are lucky enough to attend these trips, you are not only representing yourself, but also your consortia, agency, and host agency. Be the professional we all look up to and aspire to be like—not the Shrimp Lady.

STRATEGIC PLANNING

Are you living paycheck to paycheck? Did you find that, during Wave Season, you were unable to help some of your customers book their trip because the cruise or tour was sold out? This is a common complaint, especially among newer travel professionals. New agents tend to focus on what's available right now and don't plan for future needs. I was the same way when I started in retail travel sales. We opened for business in August and my very first sale was a repositioning cruise from Vancouver to Los Angeles only a month later.

I'm the first to admit when "I don't know what I don't know." I was fortunate to have a very strong BDM to mentor me in this area. Her guidance kept me from making one of the biggest mistakes I see so many agents, particularly newer ones, make: the failure to plan strategically for sales.

I get it. We've all got bills to pay, but we need to look to the future because the future is always just around the corner. The Q1 "Wave Season" gets all the attention because this is when a lot of activity takes place. People are done with the holidays and ready to plan their spring break and summer travel. However, according to some of the largest agencies in the business, September, October, and November are prime months. In fact according to one of the largest vacation agencies in the world, October (yes—October!) is traditionally their *best booking month* in terms of dollar volume, better than any other month of the year.

From a booking perspective, the fall is when you make or break your business. Suppliers will begin the initial push for their summer and fall products for the next year. As a strategic seller, you should always be thinking eight to ten months ahead. For example, high season in Alaska and Europe is July and August. Both destinations typically carry a higher price point (and commission) and require a greater time commitment from the customer. These aren't last-minute trips! Begin focusing the following year's sales efforts by blocking and selling space for those summer months—especially deluxe and luxury products such as Regent and Crystal and popular destinations like Alaska and Europe—in the preceding fall.

If you don't want to compete with the vast majority of travel agents in the world, focus on selling cruise tours. Travel professionals are doing their customers and their bank account a great injustice by not offering *every* customer the opportunity to see more—more of Alaska than the Inside Passage, more of the coastal cities in Europe, or even more of the inland region near a river cruise. A few days of touring on either end of a cruise can turn an average vacation into a once-in-a-lifetime experience for the customer—and increased commission for you.

While suppliers look at revenue generated in a calendar year, the WTA focuses on a sales or booking year of September to August. Typically, most of what you will sell in the last four months will travel the following year. As a general rule, you should have at least 60–65 percent of all your business for next year booked by the first of January. In doing so, you will be able to accurately predict cash flow so you won't scramble for last-minute sales to pay the bills. If you focus on selling last-minute Caribbean holiday travel, or anything else anyone will buy from you—you are thinking tactically. This is the equivalent of living paycheck to paycheck, and the results won't be any different. Make the commitment to a strategic future today.

How about rebating?

According to a survey by Pam Danziger in her book *Let Them Eat Cake*, the majority of consumers pay full price for luxury experiential goods—except when it comes to travel. The survey revealed that 64 percent of individuals got a discount or a deal on their last travel purchase. Consumers in all markets have been conditioned to ask retailers for discounts. However, in the travel market, the agent often *offers* a discount even before being asked.

When you are selling, *please* don't tell prospects that you will give them a discount up front or that you will beat someone else's price. Many travel agents do this because they feel guilty about asking large sums of money for a vacation. Either they don't believe in the value of the trip or they don't believe in the value of their service. Most likely both! If customers ask for a discount (and sometimes they will), then it becomes a negotiation. If you offer a discount up front, you've made their decision to purchase about the price, and you've lost before you've even begun.

As one of my customers, who became a good friend and mentor, once told me, "Danny boy, I don't mind you making money off of me, but I don't want you getting fat!" Those words still ring in my ears: provide great value at a fair price and you have a loyal customer.

If you are going to get your customers to spend six figures on a *vacation*—not a house or a car, but a *vacation*—you had better have a pretty good feeling about money and not be afraid to ask for it. Odds are pretty good that the buyer knows what the cost is, but he is not going to buy until you ask for the money. Why? Because he knows you are scared to ask for a certain amount. Will you sweat it out? It's just like anything else you do: the more practice you have, the easier it gets.

What about service fees?

Let's talk about service fees for a minute because there are a number of views on this subject. Most agents believe they are doing their customers a disservice by charging a fee for their services when they are already compensated by the vendor. Frankly, this thought process is asinine—for several reasons.

As I discussed earlier, customers *expect* a discount on travel, whether they're buying a $299 three-night cruise or a $400,000 world cruise. Unfortunately, our industry has become its own worst enemy over the years. We have always promised the customer the lowest price, even after the sale. This is driven by one emotion: fear—the fear that the customer will cancel and book with another agent or worse—book direct. Granted, this does happen, but not as often as you think. What is more common is that the agent, either by their own volition or due the customer's inquiry, will immediately call the vendor to get a lower price for the customer. That's part of the service a travel agent provides.

If you conduct business like this, you end up doing twice as much work for a lot less money because you are actually selling the same booking *twice*. Is it just me, or is there something inherently wrong with this? Your job is to make a profit for yourself and your agency so you can stay in business to serve your customers. Repeat customers are very difficult to service if you are out of business—that's the reality. I think a happy medium for everyone is one that is totally expected by the customer (and you can thank the airlines for this nugget). Charge change fees—period! You should be compensated for your extra effort, and you probably saved your customers a few bucks as well. Hell, you may even make more on the change fees than the original commission.

So I'll ask the question: what are you worth? Wealthy Travel Agents know exactly how much they are worth. They know the value they bring to the table and are very comfortable asking a customer for $100,000 or more for their vacation. They're comfortable resisting the impulse to discount every trip, and they charge change fees because they know their time is valuable.

COMPETING WITH THE BIG GUYS

Two names have come to epitomize the us-against-them attitude many travel professionals have today: Vacations To Go (VTG) and Costco Travel. If you have ever come up against them in a competitive situation, it can be rather daunting. Fear not, I will share a few insights that will help you not only be competitive, but in many cases win the business. You can do this without rebating if you have the tools.

If you are among the roughly 45 percent of agents or agencies that aren't affiliated with a host or consortia—you are at a distinct disadvantage. Both Costco and VTG negotiate deals directly with suppliers. Without the financial strength of an affiliated agency group, you will be hard-pressed to match them. But all is not lost.

Contrary to popular belief, neither Costco nor VTG is a rampant rebater. They are, however, two different animals and I will address them each individually

Vacations To Go

No question, VTG is the 5,000-pound gorilla in the industry. Their newsletter boasts millions of subscribers, offering last-minute deals on cruises and tours ranging from mass-market vacations to some of the most luxurious trips in the world. Like most major players in the channel, they draw customers from all over the world.

Based in Houston, Texas, VTG has a large, on-site call center. Although their business model is price driven, it would be a grievous error to assume VTG salespeople are drones reading from prepared scripts. Their agents are well trained in both sales and product.

Believe it or not, VTG is one of the best things to happen to the travel industry. Yes, you heard me correctly. I am sure a great many of you reading today have had a prospect reach out to you because they received the VTG newsletter and found something of interest.

Congratulations—you are the beneficiary of a precious gift. Whether the prospect is new to you or a past guest, they are viable lead. They took the initiative to call you for more information. The only problem is that they also expect you to give them the same deal VTG is offering.

No need to panic. Suppliers work closely with VTG because they can move inventory fast. They have the marketing and operational infrastructure to make this happen, and over the years it has become a well-oiled machine. As large and powerful as they are, they are really just a travel agency—albeit a very successful one. Like you, they are a part of the retail distribution system known as the "trade" channel. This channel accounts for anywhere between 50–90 percent of a given supplier's overall sales, so it is not in the supplier's best interest to risk alienating the rest of the channel by playing favorites. Most of VTG's deals are price driven, and as a result, there are very few—if any—ancillary items to deal with. This makes your job much easier, and here is how.

Many suppliers will price match for you any deal they have provided to VTG *including* the ancillary products that may be included (shipboard credit, beverage package, etc.). You need to simply call the reservations sale department and request the price match. Usually this will do the trick. If it doesn't, contact the supplier's BDM who handles your account and ask for their help.

In most cases, you do not have the resources to market to as many people as they do. Their marketing is driving business to you. The great thing is—VTG is fine with that. They are growing the trade channel which creates opportunity for everyone.

Costco and other membership clubs

In the 1990s and early 2000s, Sam's Travel Club was the driving force in member travel sales. Sam's got out of the travel business (though they have recently re-entered the arena) and currently, the dominant player in member club travel sales is Costco Travel.

It's not just the warehouse clubs competing with you for the business. It's AARP, time-share exchanges, travel clubs, multi-level marketing (MLM) companies, and others. So how can you compete? After all, they seem to have unbeatable deals that you can't touch—or can you?

First you need to understand why your prospects, even long-time customers, reach out to these organizations to begin with. Travel is not their primary product. Costco, BJ's, and Sam's all have their warehouses. AARP is a lobbying organization to help protect the rights of retired people. AAA (and CAA) are auto clubs. Travel is just one of the many benefits these and other clubs provide for their paying members.

Suppliers like these clubs because they are "closed" groups, meaning you must join in order to receive benefits. As such, they are able to offer incentives not typically available to the general public. For example, have you ever tried to book a hotel and the reservation agent asks if you are a member of AAA or AARP? The club rates are a benefit to these closed groups. Think about it—many of us are already members of these organizations. While we may not use the travel benefits, we take advantage of many other services they offer.

There are three primary reasons your prospect contacts their membership clubs:

1. *They are curious.* Travel is often featured in the club's monthly magazine or newsletter. The customers haven't paid much attention in the past, but now they are planning a vacation. They want to see what

benefits their club membership offers and how they compare to the package you offered.

2.　　*They paid for the membership.* As a paying member, they want to feel like they are getting their money's worth. I have been an American Express Platinum Cardholder for twenty-five years. Sure it, cost $650 a year, but I get shipboard credits (SBCs) when we cruise, free roadside assistance and towing, hotel upgrades, airline club membership, Global Entry reimbursement, and other benefits. I've paid for these benefits with my annual fee, and I want to feel like I am getting my money's worth by taking advantage of as many as possible. Your prospects feel the same way about their memberships.

3.　　*They were referred by friends or family.* Most of these clubs have their own call centers, or they farm the benefit out to a large travel company who "white labels" their services. In most call centers, the agents may not necessarily be well traveled, but they are very well trained. Don't ever dismiss their knowledge and service. In fact, many of your customer's friends and family may have had very good experiences with agents from these clubs. As we all know, the best prospects usually come from referrals.

Knowing why your prospects reach out to their member clubs is a big step toward understanding how to best serve them. They often don't realize that each time they call about their vacation, they will get whoever happens to pick up the phone—as opposed to someone like you, a dedicated resource focused solely on providing them with the best vacation experience possible.

There are some benefits to booking with Costco and other membership clubs, but there are also a tremendous number of benefits to working with you. You are not just a random agent the client gets when they call an 800 number. You have a one-on-one relationship with your clients and a vast network of resources to draw from to serve them. Actually, come to think of it, most travel professionals are not aware of everything in their own arsenal. Not only can they compete with big buying clubs, but they can win!

I follow a five-step system which, on the surface, appears to relatively intuitive, but it took years of trial and error to perfect. The key is to be prepared. Don't wait until you get the dreaded call to read this section. Be ready when it comes, and it *will* come.

The first step, when you get the call that begins, "I called Costco" (or insert the membership club of choice), is not to panic or over-react. In fact, you should expect to get this call every time you pick up the phone. In this business, virtually all prospects shop around for price and value. If you become defensive or speak poorly of a club's call-center agents, you will immediately lose trust with your prospect. Instead say, "That's great! I am sure you called me because of the great relationship we have. I would love the opportunity to see what I can do for you. Do you mind if I ask you a few questions?"

Which brings us to the next step, *gather as much information as possible*. Don't worry about matching the exact offer. Price will be the easiest—the value-add amenities is where you will have to do some work. Remember, an amenity is only a benefit if it is important to the prospect. Asking the right questions will help you determine what these are. Use this information to build your own benefit list that is unique to the prospect.

The third step is knowing the resources at your disposal ahead of time. This can make or break your shot at getting the sale. Be aware of all the benefits offered via your host or consortia, loyalty programs, and credit card offers, just to name a few. I think you will be surprised at what you will find when you do some research.

Next, build a comparison chart and "net out" the offers. Once you look at the offers from a value perspective, you will probably find you are much closer to the club's offer than you initially thought. In fact, you may actually provide a greater value. In my opinion, if you are within a couple of hundred dollars in net value, you are in what negotiators call the ZOPA, or zone of opportunity for agreement.

This brings me to the last and biggest variable in the system—*you*! As a travel professional, you need to make yourself an invaluable part of the overall vacation experience. It is important to know how to sell yourself, communicate your value, and leverage your relationships. You may need to remind the customer how valuable their vacation time really is. Do they want to trust this asset to the lowest bidder (to be fair, some will), or do they want an experienced travel professional who is with them every step of the way?

Most people don't want the cheapest price; they want to make sure they are getting a great value. You can make the difference between an average experience or one they will always remember—for the right reasons.

TAKING CARE OF YOUR CUSTOMER

There are two types of customer care. The first is the kind you're probably thinking of: how you treat customers while they're purchasing from you. This includes how we interact with customers in a typical transaction—we'll call that your standard service—and how we interact when a transaction is complicated, stressful, or just plain screwed up! The second type of customer care is more subtle, and a lot of agents forget about it completely. It's how we treat customers when they're *between* purchases. This type of care is how customers are retained between transactions. It also drives referrals because you're the first name on their lips when they think of travel or vacations.

Customer service

Sometimes no matter how well we prepare and practice, things go wrong. I recently hosted a webcast to share my e-learning program, "Secrets of Selling to the Affluent Traveler." We had over 400 people from all over the world register for the event. It was supposed to be an hour of sharing the highlights of the program—useful information students could put to use immediately to transform their business.

I logged in to the webinar provider and gave what I thought was one of my best performances. I delivered the program with the sincere passion that I have for helping travel professionals like you reach the level of success they desire.

The problem was—no one listening. Unbeknownst to me, the webinar provider had conducted an update which caused a database error that did not allow registered users log in. In short, the program failed because my audience couldn't watch it! However, while I was broadcasting, all appeared to be running fine—that is, until I signed off and checked my e-mail. Yikes! Let's just say that my customers were not satisfied!

We are so dependent on technology that this can happen to any of us. It may be as simple as a storm severing your internet connection, or it could be a complete system breakdown like I experienced. My webinar provider is used by some of the most successful speakers and coaches in the field, and it usually works perfectly. But when I needed it, it failed to deliver.

How you handle these difficult situations will make all the difference in the world to your customers. I used customer service skills I practiced years ago while working on cruise ships.

Here is what I did.

I apologized and expressed gratitude. I made sure every customer knew how much I appreciated them. Once I did this, the tone of the e-mails I was received turned from anger and frustration to gratitude and understanding. I learned that my readers and students are hungry for real, actionable information that can help transform their lives and businesses. I am fortunate to be in a position to help. It is a responsibility I never take for granted.

I acknowledged the situation. As soon as I gained access to the registration list, I immediately sent an e-mail to acknowledge the problem. I didn't try to put a spin on it—I told the truth. My students took time out of their busy schedules to attend the webcast. Many took their lunch hour or time away from work. To me, the failed webinar was the same as a client not showing up for an appointment. It was very frustrating—for all of us.

I accepted full responsibility. My students signed up to learn from me. That didn't happen. The fact that the technology provider I contracted with failed to deliver still makes it my responsibility.

I offered options. Fortunately, the breakdown was with the database portion of the program and not with the webinar broadcast itself. I had the recording, and a link was sent to all registered users within a few hours to review the webinar at their leisure. Many of the customers did so.

I also scheduled a "make-up" date for those who still wanted to attend the event. I had to do the presentation all over again. Yes, I did twice as much work to make these customers happy, but I was glad to do it. As a result, they were satisfied. They could tell that I genuinely cared about them and their success.

Things can and will go wrong in your business, often at the worst times. How you deal with it will ultimately determine whether your customers will choose to do business with you or find someone else.

Customer retention

Have you ever been in a relationship where you get the feeling the other person really doesn't care about you as much as they say they do? I love Delta Airlines, but that's not how I think Delta feels about me. Contrary to what former Delta CEO Richard Anderson says in their inflight safety video, I question how much Delta really does care about its customers—especially a long-time, loyal passenger like me.

In the past two years I have flown over 125,000 miles per year, qualifying me for the highest level of their customer loyalty program. I am close to becoming a Delta Million Miler—which brings me to the point of all of this. It's not a complaint, although at times it may sound like one, but more of an observation and lesson about the real reason most people take their business to a different vendor. Between January and June 2015, I did not board a single Delta aircraft. Prior to that, I averaged 7500 flown miles a month for 10 years. Now, let that sink in for a minute. That is an average of 90,000 miles a year for over a decade.

What would you do if one of your top customers, someone you did business with once a week or so, one of your most loyal patrons suddenly disappeared? My guess is you would first check the obituaries to see if the customer had died! When that turned up a negative, you would check other resources. If you were Delta, for example, you could check the activity on my Delta American Express card. If they had checked my card activity, they would know I was not dead. I was very much alive and spending up a storm on their co-branded card!

Maybe they could have simply picked up the phone and called to see if everything was ok. This is exactly what American Express did when the account activity on my Business Platinum card, which I have had since 1994, became almost nonexistent (due to the Delta Sky Miles Gold Card). American Express showed me the love. They cared.

To this day, I have not heard from any of the fine people at Delta (I mean this sincerely—their service people are the best) regarding my sudden disappearance. Did I hit the lottery and buy a NetJets card, or did I make a career change that allows me to pick and choose when I travel? Did I switch loyalty to of their competitors? Did I move away from a Delta hub? They have no idea because they've never asked.

I live in Seattle, a city rich in aerospace history, and there is an old saying here: "If it ain't Boeing, I ain't going!" That's how I have always felt about Delta. I can't remember my wife's cell phone number for the life of me, but I could recite my Delta Sky Miles number while in a coma if asked. I earned the nickname "Delta Dan" at my last place of employment because I was usually willing to pay the cost difference to keep from flying rival carriers. Now, you might think my blind loyalty was misguided. Just the opposite is true. They took good care of me. Once I reached the exalted status of Diamond and Platinum, the travel experience on any other carrier was simply intolerable. I imagine AA and United elite feel the same way when forced on a different airline. I just don't like turning into a pumpkin. In the end, what does it mean to be a loyal

Delta customer? For me, as much as I love Delta, it's time to face reality and start playing the field.

If one of your top customers simply vanished, I bet that you would want to find out why. If nothing else, reaching out simply shows your concern and your appreciation of their business. I guess Delta will never know why I stopped flying because they are too indifferent to ask. There you have it, the real reason most people choose to leave a business to which they have been loyal —indifference.

The lesson is one of fundamental customer service. Follow up, let your customer know you care. Don't just say it—show them the love. If they go away for a while, reach out and ask why. You might just learn something.

CALL TO ACTION

Most people are not willing to implement what they learn and as a result, nothing changes. What strategic changes are you going to make to better serve your business?

1. *Decide your business model.* Choose the skills and specialization that will add value to your transactions for your customer *and* your supplier. Remember, you can't be all things to all people.

2. *Practice to become an expert.* Whether you use my coat hook method to master product or

another method, learn the itineraries and accommodations for at least two brands.

3. *Experience the product.* Take FAM trips to your region of specialty and invest time in learning about a region via websites, print, and video. Your customers want insider information and your own experiences will be an asset when you're making recommendations.

4. *Choose your partners wisely.* Research hosts and suppliers. Learn the benefits and costs of each option and choose the one that adds the most value to your business.

5. *Make a strategic sales plan.* What are you selling right now? Are your booking for next month or next year? Aim to make 60 percent or more of the next year's bookings by January 1. Plan your sales and marketing efforts eight to ten months ahead to accurately predict cash flow.

6. *Commit to providing exceptional customer care.* If you haven't had an exceptional customer care experience, seek one out. Visit a business known for its high level of service. Visit several! Take notes. How can you give each of your customers the same high level of service before, during, and after they purchase travel from you?

Chapter 4
The Wealthy Travel Agent
Sales System

People are not born with great sales skills—they are developed over time. A salesperson may have started picking up some of these skills at a very young age by observing a parent or grandparent in the sales business. If Grandpa was an ethical, customer-focused salesperson, these organically acquired skills can be an asset. But if he was consistently unethical (think the stereotypical used-car salesperson who would lie, cheat, or steal to get you in a car) the child may pick up bad sales habits. It's tougher to unlearn bad habits than it is to learn a good sales process. It's worth it to approach sales with intention—as a specific process rather than as a loose collection of attempts to convince a customer to purchase a product or service.

113

When I was a teenager, I bought a book with my very own money for the first time. It was *How to Sell Anything to Anybody* by Joe Girard. At that time, he was in the *Guinness Book of World Records* as the "Greatest Salesperson in the World." Joe sold Chevys. That in itself is not significant. What is? The world's greatest salesperson sold Chevys—in, of all places, Detroit. As the car-manufacturing capital of the world at the time, Detroit was also the most difficult sales market in the world. In a city where buyers were fiercely loyal to their brands, Joe managed to sell more than anyone.

How did he do it? Joe developed a systematic process from prospecting to follow up. This is something common to virtually all successful salespeople—they have a process. Mine might be different than Joe's, and yours may be different than mine, but the basic mechanics of the process are the same.

Since we are on the subject of automobiles, I like to go car-shopping with my wife. For one, I know that, although what's hers is hers, what's mine is ours. But more importantly, she has a hypersensitive BS detector—and very little patience for the person spewing it. She doesn't want to feel like someone is trying to constantly convince her to make a purchase. On the other hand, when I am ready to buy, I like to seek out a salesperson. I am usually pretty good at finding one who knows what he is talking about and puts my interests ahead of his own.

Confidence is the first product of a systematic sales process. A process instills confidence in the salesperson and, more importantly, in the customer. This buyer confidence is very important, especially when selling to affluent customers. Affluent buyers, more than anyone, want to buy a product, not be sold on it. A knowledgeable, confident salesperson will gain the respect of a prospective buyer almost immediately. Confidence puts the buyer at ease, and the buying process becomes more and more of a consultation as trust grows.

Preparation is a key step in the sales process. You have probably heard the expression "Winning is 80 percent preparation and 20 percent perspiration." This is especially true in sales. Preparation allows you to control the sales process, and control is key to closing the sale. When the conversation gets way off track, control allows you to bring it back to any place in the process you like—and you can't have this kind of control without preparation. You must know your pitch backward, forward, and out of order. In fact, I suggest that you have your sales talk scripted and memorized, or at the very least in bulleted talking points, and practice to the point that it sounds like a natural conversation to the prospective buyer.

I am going to go out on a limb and assume we've all been pulled over for speeding. Remember how the conversation went? The officer asked carefully scripted questions, and you answered. There probably wasn't idle chitchat because the officer controlled the conversation. It's a very similar situation when you're selling travel. Be prepared, have a well-rehearsed script, and ask a lot of questions. Let the prospect do most of the talking—75 percent them to 25 percent you is a good ratio. It is important in any sales situation for the salesperson to maintain control of the process, just like a police offer controls the conversation during a traffic stop.

When control is relinquished to the prospect, it almost always results in a lost sale. We all know what it feels like to lose control of a sales situation. The prospect tells you how to do your job, where to find the information, and how to negotiate the price. And then they get up from their chair or hang up the phone, and you never hear from them again.

You are responsible for driving the process, not the customer. Lead the conversation without allowing for unrelated tangents. When the inevitable does occur, your knowledge of your sales system will help you pick up right where you got sidetracked.

CHOOSING YOUR CUSTOMERS

Your customers are your partners, so choose them carefully. The biggest struggle of any business is how to find new potential customers, also known as prospects. Simply the thought of prospecting strikes fear in the hearts of salespeople everywhere. I mean, shouldn't marketing drive new prospects? That's not your department, is it? Let's not be naïve. As the

CEO and CTC (chief toilet cleaner) of your business, you have responsibility for everything, including prospecting. Prospecting should receive the resources it deserves—it is the lifeblood of your business. There are a number of gurus who throw around numbers as to how much it costs to acquire or keep a customer, and we could argue it until the cows come home. The exact number doesn't matter. You have to prospect. If you don't, your business will starve for customers.

Right now you are probably selling anything to anyone who will buy from you, so it may be difficult to decide where you should spend your resources. But it doesn't have to be that way. Before you go off and spend a bunch of time and money on prospecting, doesn't it make sense to decide who *you* want to do business with, instead of the other way around?

Personally, I don't want to deal with people who are only looking for the cheapest price and will beat you up over a single dollar. Screw that! I want buyers who value the service and expertise I bring to the table. I am sure you feel the same way. Remember, your customers are not just buying a vacation. They're getting you, too! You are a critical part of the overall experience—you provide added value because of your knowledge, training, and professionalism.

Imagine your ideal customer. Think about who this person is. Let's use the previous example of river cruising. Who wants to sail up rivers around the world? Well, there are a lot of people who do—so which ones do you want? River cruise experiences are like ocean cruises in that you can travel at a variety of price points on vessels with a variety of amenities. Try not to think of your customer in terms of demographics, though. Think lifestyle—are they active, social, intellectual? What types of experiences will they want to enjoy: art, music, history, food, sports, spa? Paint a picture of who they are. Once you have a vivid picture it will be easy to position your services to attract new, ideal customers.

But what about your existing clients? Guess what—you don't have to keep them on your top client list, even if they are regulars. I'm not saying that you should dump your whole database and start from scratch, but you have a business to run, and you should make sure the customers you choose to keep are truly profitable. Sometimes the ones you think are profitable might not be. Take a look at your regulars to make sure you are not just breaking even or losing money on their transactions. This boils down to a trade-off: how much is your time worth? High-maintenance world cruises with commissions in the $10,000–$40,000 range are ones you can afford to service—and need to service—at a very high level. The $200–$300 commission customers are your "bread and butter" and shouldn't take as much of your time. But don't lose sight of the fact that their vacation is just as important to them as world cruise is to the luxury client.

I once had an agent working with us who just did not get it. She would spend hours with a customer who she *knew* only booked the one-night repositioning cruise from Seattle to Vancouver. Really, you can't make this stuff up. In fact, I still have one of the commission checks packed away somewhere—I never cashed it! Why would I? It was the lowest I had ever seen. The one-night cruise for two people was over $200. The commissionable amount was just $5 per person. The rest went to port taxes and government fees. The commission, with the consortia override, came to a whopping $1.40! I figured it probably cost more to cut and mail the check than it was worth. I was told by our BDM that we were lucky to get the check—if it is less than a dollar they don't bother sending it.

Who do you fire in this situation? Not the cruise line. They had to move the ship to Vancouver for the Alaska season and were basically giving the trip away. The answer is both the agent *and* the customer. This was not an isolated incident, and it exemplifies the real difference between being a travel agent and a sales person. The agent (who worked on commission) was stupid to spend so much time on the booking. That's obvious. But the customer got fired as well. They were not, nor would they ever be, a meaningful contributor to our cash flow. I have heard the argument that trips like this introduce new guests to cruising, almost like a FAM trip for the customer. But I have been around long enough to know that these people will rarely book anything else, so I would recommend referring them, either to a competitor you want to see go out of business or—better yet—directly to the vendor.

In the 1990s, my travel agency was one of the largest sellers of Commodore Cruise Line in the United States. My guess is most of you have never heard of them. They eventually went bankrupt in 2001, and we very well might have, too, if we hadn't examined our margins on their products.

Commodore's seven-day cruise package out of New Orleans was priced at $399 (inside), $499 (ocean view), and $599 (suite). This was pre-9/11 and at that time most Caribbean cruises sailed from South Florida, so to have a ship that was only a five-hour drive away from our Texas city made it an easy sell. However, at that price point, it attracted mostly first-time cruisers and inexperienced travelers. Many had saved for months to afford this vacation and needed a lot of hand-holding. We were selling a ton of it, but something was wrong. We were starting to have trouble paying the bills.

After reviewing several months of transactional data, I determined that each Commodore sale took an average of four hours to research, sell, and service—*twice* as long as a normal booking. Even at 20 percent commission, we were losing $125 per sale. We immediately "fired" the cruise line and began referring the customers to other suppliers. Not a lot of them booked, but that was OK. It allowed us to refocus our resources on profitable customers and products.

It is easy to fall into the "sales volume" trap. Your BDMs are paid on sales volume so you will be encouraged to produce as much as possible. But what is good for them is not necessarily good for you. Pay attention to this lesson—it is one of the most important takeaways from this book. It's not about how much you sell, but what you have left in your pocket at the end of the day that counts.

When you are calculating profitability or lifetime value (LTV) of customers and suppliers, never, ever forget that this is *your* business, and it does not pay to keep any relationships that don't contribute to its ongoing success. Don't be afraid to turn them loose. That said, you have to be diligent to keep the relationships that *are* profitable. You may have fewer customers, but you'll make more money—I am sure you don't have a problem with that.

Sports teams do this all the time. If a player is not producing, they are either sent down to the minors or cut loose altogether. It may sound cruel, but the success of the team is the priority. It will pay dividends to think this way about your business.

Attracting new customers with a higher LTV is one way to increase profits. The other way is to increase the LTV of your current clients—but how? In my experience, the average travel-agency customer takes three vacations annually: a cruise, a land-based vacation, and a trip to see Grandma and Grandpa. Assuming you currently book one of their trips, cruise or land, capturing the other will take you from one-third to two-thirds of their vacation spending. You don't really care about the trip to the grandparents, but the second vacation can double revenue for you. It should be an easy sale since they already entrust you with one vacation. Why not both? They might book both with you if you have a strong relationship with them. However, if they want a complicated fully independent traveler (FIT) air/car/hotel package and you don't have the skills or resources to fulfill their request, it may be hard to obtain and maintain the extra trip each year.

It is likely is that your customer will, at some point, choose to leave you. When I was with Cruise Holidays, we asked our franchisees how much of their business was repeat. The typical answer ranged from 50–60 percent. However, after analyzing the data from their own point of sale (POS) system, the number of customers that booked two or more times with the same agent or agency was actually less than 30 percent. These customers didn't stop taking vacations—they just stopped booking with that agent or agency. And the reason they left? The agents assumed that because of their "exemplary service and low prices" that the customers would always come back. When we surveyed the ex-customers, the number one reason they'd left was "indifference." The reality is, if the agents had made an effort to communicate with the customers on a regular basis, they might have retained them.

FINDING NEW CUSTOMERS

The biggest challenge you will face in your business is finding new qualified prospects for your sales funnel. We are going to look at a couple of methods that have worked for me and many others who specialize in this demographic. Start close to home with your own customer and prospect database. Your database is the real key to your success. Treat it like gold! It is the most valuable asset, other than *you*, that your business has.

Do you simply have a list of names and e-mail addresses, or maybe postal addresses, that you've accumulated? Perhaps you bought a list or acquired a club membership list or two along the way. However you got them—you need to know who these people are.

When I decided to focus on selling deluxe and luxury products, I knew I needed to learn as much about my customers as I possibly could. To start, my database was about 10,000 names: mostly purchased lists, several club membership lists, past customers, and prospects—basically a hodgepodge of junk.

The challenge was to go through every single name in the database and input as much information as I possibly could about them. Not just name, address, phone number, and e-mail address—but what kind of car do they drive, where do they work? How much money do they make? How many kids do they have? How old are the kids and where do they go to school? What types of vacation experiences have they had in the past? What are their interests? Anything I could learn went into their profiles.

By the time I finished the process, the list contained fewer than 2500 names, but I knew something about virtually every one of them— including the fact that they were still alive (don't laugh, it happens). I was able to target our local marketing which saved a significant amount of money, but also the consortia support as well. Not only was the cleaned-up database an asset to the business, but suppliers were more willing to spend co-op because they knew it was possible to target specific prospects. The end result was that marketing expenses decreased dramatically. Sales and profits skyrocketed. Why? I defined my prospects, learned about them, and told them about products that mattered to them and some that no one else was proactively selling,

Take care of your database the way a Marine cares for his rifle: love it, clean it, nurture it—your life depends on it.

Social media

Social media is a great tool to connect to with clientele and build relationships. You need to get savvy with all the ways that your customers want to communicate: e-mail, instant messaging, texting, and social media. The time for the phone calls is over with this upcoming generation.

You're going to hear the stories like "I posted a deal on Facebook, and I made a $10,000 sale." Well, I'm not going to say that that doesn't happen. Occasionally—very occasionally—things like that do happen, just like in Silicon Valley, occasionally companies like Facebook go public and turn their twenty-five-year-old founders into billionaires. What you don't hear about are the tens of thousands of tech start-ups that end up in bankruptcy or just kind of plugging along out there. Not everybody hits a home run.

According to a survey by the Keller-Fay Group and featured by Wharton marketing professor Jonah Burger in his 2013 book *Contagious: Why Things Catch On,* only a small fraction of word-of-mouth marketing is online. Some studies claim the number is as low as 5 percent.

According to Radius Global, Millennials ranked word-of-mouth as the number one influencer in their purchasing decisions about clothes, packaged goods, big-ticket items (like travel and electronics), and financial products. Baby Boomers also ranked word-of-mouth as being most influential in their purchasing decisions about big-ticket items and financial products.

Contrary to popular belief, social media should not be your big bet to grow your business, but it is a way to build your reputation and credibility in the community which will have a greater effect in positioning your expertise.

Social media is a tool to help your business communicate with prospects and clients. There are a lot of choices out there with social-media platforms. What are they? Well, you have LinkedIn, which is a business platform. You have Facebook, Pinterest, Instagram, Google Plus, and Twitter, not to mention SnapChat and Periscope. What are you going to do? If you engage with customers on every social-media platform that's out there, you'll never have time to sell anything! You need to make money so that you can continue to serve your customers. Decide how involved you're going to be on social media; pick just one or two platforms to put your time into. The platforms you choose should be the places where your target customer is hanging out!

You won't see me posting too frequently on my social media accounts. People who post constantly are either are not devoting enough time to building their business, or they are large enough to hire employees or companies that are dedicated to managing their social media. They don't do it all themselves. If you're the CEO and CTC, investigate products like Hootsuite to help save you time and money. They have a free version that allows you to post to several social-media platforms simultaneously.

For my business, I focus on LinkedIn. I'm in the business of developing sales leaders and helping people grow their businesses, so I develop my network within the most business-oriented platform—LinkedIn.

Why? Well, it's simple. People are much more receptive to becoming friends with people they don't know well (acquaintances) if it may benefit them or their business at a later date. Through my LinkedIn account, I've referred many "friends" to travel agents who specialize in the destination they are interested in visiting. They have referred me to other business associates looking for speaking or consulting services. It's kind of a tit-for-tat relationship on LinkedIn, as opposed to a more chatty and personal social-media site like Facebook.

Should you choose LinkedIn as your focus? Sure, why not? You are in the business of selling vacation products. People who are in business take vacations. I would choose LinkedIn as my social-media venue to grow my travel business as well as my coaching business. The real question is: are you likely to use it? And are your customers there? It really comes down to the platform you prefer and the platform your target customers prefer. Ideally you'll find a site or app that covers both those bases.

Block out fifteen to twenty minutes a day and devote yourself to your social media. When you're done, step away from it. You don't want it to consume you. You need to spend your time building your business. Set a social-media budget so that you can post ad programs on Facebook and LinkedIn.

LinkedIn and Facebook ad campaigns are a great way to advertise your abilities on a small budget.

I am going to let you in on a little secret and it was Anthony Bourdain who helped me see it clearly. *Some of the most successful sellers of travel spend the least amount of time in their office.*

You know who they are. They frequently post or tweet their enviable experiences as they travel the world. I mean really, with all that gallivanting across continents, how do they run—much less grow—their businesses? The obvious tools such as laptops, smart phones, and free hotel Wi-Fi come to mind, and there are other portable business tools as well. However, the real answer lies within.

The fact that they travel frequently is a primary driver of customers to their business model. *They embrace travel as a lifestyle and* **attract customers through the sheer act of traveling.** Their clients (and many of us professionals) live vicariously through their exploits on Facebook, Instagram, and Twitter. They have become professional travelers, and this makes them especially attractive to potential clients.

Put yourself in the client's shoes for a minute. Would you rather work with an agent who you have seen posting recently from a destination, or one who sits behind a desk talking about what it was like to be there five years ago? The answer is obvious.

As you know, I am the biggest advocate in the business for professional education. However, these globe-trotting agents take it to a whole new level.

They are using their travels to gain specialized knowledge and the credibility of recent experience, and they're letting the world know about it via social media to attract customers. This is powerful.

Think about your own sales after you have been on a FAM or new vacation experience. There is almost always a spike in sales for that cruise line, tour company, or destination. Now imagine that you are traveling once a month or more and the inevitable spikes that will follow—travel is good for business and it's good for social-media engagement.

If you are like most of us, with obligations that prevent frequent travel, you can emulate their success by posting photos and comments of your most recent travels (the last year or so is okay). Use the "drip method" to keep your followers interested. Posting a little bit each week on your website, blog, or newsletter, you can easily stretch a weeklong trip into four to eight weeks of posts. Each post can highlight a different service, amenity, landmark, activity, or meal—from a traveler's perspective.

Our customers are also our social-media followers. They are a selfish lot and want regular new content. The good news? They're following us because they're interested in travel. They don't just want to know about offers and packages they can purchase, they also want to see us experiencing travel for travel's sake. Let's give them what they want and everyone wins!

Dynamic prospecting systems

Have you ever had a close friend or family member ask you to help plan a vacation for them? You help them find the perfect package for their needs—and then you never hear from them, only to find out they booked it with someone they hardly know (or direct). You spent a lot of time and effort with nothing to show for it. Did you wonder why they did this?

Stanford University sociologist Mark Granovetter conducted a groundbreaking study in the 1970s about how people get jobs. In his study, Granovetter found that people rarely found jobs in the newspaper or other resources available at the time—and it wasn't because a close friend or relative helped them get a job, either. He found most people got jobs through acquaintances, or what he called "weak ties."

Granovetter describes the bulk of the job creation taking place through acquaintances. That is, people mostly find jobs from friends of friends, or relatives of friends, or via relationships even more removed! The study, "The Strength of Weak Ties," is considered one of the most influential of the twentieth century and its findings have been successfully applied to a number of other social situations. Malcolm Gladwell referred to it in his book *The Tipping Point*, as did Charles Duhigg in *The Power of Habits*.

How does the theory of weak ties apply to the business of selling? Great question. When you're searching for new customers, isn't that the same thing as looking for a new job? You're looking for someone to hire you to book their vacation. I have applied this principle for the past fifteen years in various roles and found it to be extremely successful in finding new customers. Why? Because it's focused on developing relationships with people that you don't know well—your weak ties.

The strong tie is someone who is in your immediate circle of influence. The weak tie is an acquaintance or someone you have never met but has a strong tie to someone who is close to you. Let's look at how you can use this theory to build your network of prospective customers.

Imagine you are invited to a dinner party at the home of your best customer. We'll call her Renee. There are seven other people invited whom you don't know and one you met one time at a previous party. These people are all good friends of Renee, but new to you. Renee is your strong tie and the rest of the guests are your weak ties. Now, during the dinner conversation one of the guests, Nate, tells you about a friend of his, Ernie, who is a dentist and is just starting to plan a vacation. Still with me? Great!

Nate gives you Ernie's telephone number and offers to make an introduction. A couple of days later, you call Ernie. You chat and he books his vacation with you. Whew! What just happened? Well,

I'll tell you—and it's really simple when you think about it. Renee introduced you to Nate, who introduced you to Ernie. Renee is your level-one, your closest circle. Nate is your second-level tie, and Ernie is your third-level. Levels two and three are weak ties—you do not know them well, but Renee does.

Now it should all make sense. The first level of contacts—the Renees—are only responsible for about 10-15 percent of your sales.

Remember the family member who milked you for information and booked elsewhere? Here's why: people close to you (strong ties) do not want to risk their relationship with you and are more comfortable doing business with someone they hardly know (weak tie).

Your second-level and third-level ties will account for about 60–65 percent of your sales. The remaining balance of business (from fourth-level ties and beyond) diminishes rapidly from there, but that's OK because we know where the sweet spot is, and we are going to focus all of our efforts to get to those second- and third-level contacts.

How do you do this? It's easy. Who knows those second- and third-level people? That's right, Renee does! Reach out to your existing customers, friends, and co-workers, and ask this open-ended question: *"I am considering taking on a few new qualified clients. Who do you know that would be interested in learning about exciting vacation opportunities? Do you mind providing me with their contact information and reaching out to let them know I will be calling to visit with them?"*

A referral from your level-one gives you credibility, and your contacts are usually happy to help. Why? Because you are not asking *them* to buy anything! It's the ultimate in network marketing.

Reaching out to your weak ties is how you can grow your business, with the customers you choose, and it costs virtually nothing. You can send an e-mail as an introduction and follow up with a phone call, but it's essential that you create a conversation so that you can grow the relationship with those prospects. As they become your loyal customers, a second-level tie grows into a first-level tie, and the process starts all over again. This is the real beauty of the strength of weak ties.

Remember, affluent people tend to be loyal. You take care of them, you do a good job for them, you become friends with them, and they'll be your customer for life. That's where you get that long-term value.

Invest in your customers

Let's focus now on cultivating relationships. Find that core group of influencers and become friends with them. As part of normal conversation and getting to know people—playing golf with them or having drinks—talk about their travel habits. Everybody likes to talk about their travels because it's part of their life experience, and it's fun. Travel is a fun product. We sell fun.

Make travel part of your normal conversation. Be conscious of the strength of weak ties and use them to expand your sphere of influence. Look beyond the person in front of you. Truly resist the temptation to focus on your immediate circle of influence or that first level of contacts as prospects. You know what? They'll buy from you when the time is right. If you build strong relationships and trust with them, they will connect you with those second- and third-level ties that will be the majority of your sales. The credibility and connection you have with your first-level ties will lead to introductions to new people who can potentially become your customers. Focus your efforts on reaching those weak ties by developing strong ties, first-level connections, with people who have ties with your target customers.

People buy from people they like—don't be obnoxious. One of the characteristics of the affluent traveler is that they are socially active, so it makes sense for you to be the same. Be a joiner, become part of their crowd. Get involved with social clubs, charities, and the arts. Try to reach out to each of the different types of affluent travelers you want to attract to your business.

You are systematically building relationships, but be genuine. These first-level ties will be your friends. You want to be involved with people who are like-minded. Creating rapport by sharing something in common is the easiest way to start genuine relationships. There are a number of organizations and sports activities that you can join, but keep something in mind: when you're looking at joining a group or activity, focus on ones that will connect you with potential clients. We all have own personal causes that we support, whether we get any business out of them or not. That's OK, too—go with your heart.

CALL TO ACTION PART 1

It's time to take action and work on developing relationships with your prospects and customers.

Make a list of all the professional, social, and charitable organizations that are important to you. Pick out a couple that you really want to be involved with, that inspire you, and that you are going to gain some personal satisfaction from because you're going to be active in these organizations. Choose something that you like, but ensure that it's going to provide a healthy base of clients for you.

Now, back up and go over your current database. I want you to put together a survey. You can use a free product like Survey Monkey. Ask questions like these:

- When was your last vacation?
- Where would you like to go next?
- Have you ever taken a European or Asian river cruise and if so, what line?

- Are you interested in taking a world cruise or a segment of a world cruise?

Part of this survey strategy is to suggest things to the customer. Maybe you're reminding them that they haven't taken a vacation in a while. You're offering ideas about where they could go next and what's potentially out there that they may not have considered. How many people really know about river cruising? Maybe they think cruises are all midnight buffets and parties in the Caribbean. You can educate them by asking them questions, so they realize that there are very educational and enriching experiences available on a cruise. In fact, there are a number of amazing places that can only be accessed by cruise ship—do your customers know about them? Do they know that many people take segments of a world cruise before they graduate to the full world cruise? You need to ask them these questions. Your questions should (1) prompt their interest in vacations or vacation products, and (2) let them know that you offer those products. That's equally as important.

If you get 5–10 percent return-rate on the survey, that's great. What you're going to do is send that survey out for a second time a couple of weeks later. You're going to get another 5–10 percent response. You're going to send it out roughly six to eight times over the course of a quarter. Surveying your current database is a great way to do to keep up with your clients, too. And I have something for you to do while you're waiting for your survey results to come in.

Make a list of everybody you know in your first-level contacts—your direct circle of influence. Make sure these are people that you know very well and whose business you want (or already have).

Then, create a list of those weak ties you have met through your first-level contacts. Whether they are from social media or social events, write them down. Remember, don't try to sell to them right away, but rather reach out and work on forming a connection.

Here's your challenge: work on this section. Take some time to get it done before you move on to learning the selling process. If you have these action items completed, you'll be able to implement what you learn in the next section right away!

THE WTA SALES PROCESS

The sales process I am about to share is a simple one. There is no need to complicate a process when it works fine as it is. This is the same tried-and-true process I have used for years to produce millions of dollars in commissions, fees, and bonuses. It has worked for me and I am confident it will work for you, as long as you trust in and follow the system.

Rapport – create commonality

Rapport is simply a commonality between two people. As salespeople, our livelihood depends on rapport. If we can't quickly establish commonality with our prospect, the rest of the process will be an exercise in futility. Always remember this simple thing and you will be fine: people buy from people they like—so don't give them a reason not to like you.

There are two types of rapport, physical and verbal. Physical rapport is probably the easiest to recognize because you can see what the prospect is doing. How is he sitting? Where is he looking—or not looking? Reading eye movement can be like reading a great novel because it can tell you so much. If he looks up and to the right, he is interested. If he looks down in any direction, we might as well pack our bags and head home—it isn't going to happen.

When people think of physical rapport, the practice of "mirroring" immediately comes to mind. The practice has been the butt of jokes for years, but let me tell you—it works.

Remember, as salespeople, we want to control the process as much as possible. Lead with your body language so the prospect will mirror you. People do this subconsciously. When I meet with a prospect, whether on their turf, mine, or neutral ground like a coffee shop, I pay close attention to how they are sitting and where they are looking. I will typically lean back in my seat and adopt a relaxed, open posture.

This usually puts prospects at ease and they will do the same. We have a nice conversation; I ask questions focused on finding more commonality between us. When I am ready to get down to business, I sit up in my chair and lean forward on the desk or table. Naturally, the prospects do the same. When I want them to relax again I lean back, away from the table. Try practicing this technique on with your family or friends until it becomes natural.

Verbal rapport is important, too. The tone of your voice can be very effective. Matching tones with a prospect and then controlling the level can be very powerful when you're making a sales pitch.

When I was working the Purser's Desk on a cruise ship, we often had to deal with passengers who would get quite upset if services or accommodations were not exactly as they expected. The Purser's Desk is like the reception desk in a hotel, except our passenger couldn't simply check out and go to the hotel down the street. We needed to gain control of the situation. I learned about verbal rapport from listening to Tony Robbins cassette tapes. It became my specialty and I actually practiced these techniques on our upset guests. It would go something like this.

Guest (in a loud voice): "I am very dissatisfied with my accommodations. We are never sailing this line again, blah blah blah."

Dan (in a loud voice in the same tone and decibel level): "Yes sir, I understand you are very upset."

Then, I'd finish with quiet and calm tone. "Please allow me to help find a solution to the problem."

Usually it worked on the first try. Simply by matching and then changing the tone of my voice, I'd gain control of the situation. If they were really pissed off, I sometimes had to repeat the process two or three times, but ultimately, it worked, and the passenger was able to have a rational conversation about the situation.

This technique works on the telephone as well. It is important to listen to the tone of the caller, reflect it, and change your tone to the one you desire for the conversation. Even normal social conversations can be controlled by tone.

We all use e-mail and text messages in our daily lives, but creating physical and verbal rapport through these mediums can be difficult. I suggest you stay away from text messages when communicating with prospects. Texting is still a personal form of communication, so it is best to wait until you have a solid relationship established with your prospect and they have given permission for you to communicate via text messaging or Facebook Messenger.

When you use e-mail, be yourself. This is more useful as a relationship-building vehicle, whether a direct response from you or an auto-responder. I personally do not find e-mail very effective in creating rapport. I am also of the belief that if someone is not willing to give you a telephone number or speak with you directly, they are simply gathering price quotes and will probably go with the lowest. As a WTA, this is not a prospect you want to waste time with.

Qualify – why, why, why?

Ask questions. Get the basics. Picture a funnel: at the top of the conversation, you ask very broad questions, drilling it down so that when you get to the bottom, only one or two options pop out. In simpler terms, qualifying is asking a number of questions to determine the how, what, why, when, and where so you can help the prospect choose the product that will deliver the best experience for their needs.

The obvious questions are how many people will be traveling, where they want to go, and when. They not-so-obvious question is the *why*. This question is where you start proving your value as a sales professional. Uncovering the *why* reveals the emotional connection the prospect has to the product you are selling. That's what you are looking for.

For example, today's Boomer travelers are products of the '60s and '70s. They are the Woodstock generation. We, and I say that as a product of the last year of the Boomer generation, are looking to reconnect with the memories and experiences of our youth. For some that means traveling to the UK to walk across Abbey Road, for others it may be a visit to Southeast Asia, a region they fell in love with during a very different time. Boomers are looking to reconnect with themselves.

This reason alone may account for the surge in popularity of wellness vacations.

Once you understand all the particulars and the emotional connection to the trip, it's time to research options. Assuming you have asked all the right questions, you should be able to easily come up with a few options that meet your prospect's criteria. But just because there are multiple options doesn't mean you should share them all. In my experience, you should pick two, but then select the one you believe best fits their needs—after all, isn't this your job, to evaluate needs and solve the problem? You'll present the best option, but keep the other in your back pocket, just in case.

Presentation – selling the "sizzle"

When presenting options to prospects, we need to think like an artist. We must paint a vivid picture of the experience and emotionally tie the customer to the scene. It is so obvious, but very few agents embrace this concept of experiential selling. The reason most don't is simple. They are conditioned to sell products, whether it is a car, a home, a candy bar, or a cruise. Case in point, I receive an average of ten webinar invites per day to attend a product or destination webinar. Virtually none of them teach us travel sales professionals *how* to sell their product. The pitch is always about remodeled rooms, space ratios, square footage, and beach frontage—not about how it will make a customer feel.

Have you ever stayed at a Westin hotel? They have, by design, a very distinct scent when you walk in. They are creating an experience that appeals to all senses and creates an emotional connection to the brand. I now expect this every time I stay in a Westin, which happens to be my hotel of choice when traveling on business. In fact, on a recent trip, my wife and I stayed at the Westin Airport in Atlanta. I am so conditioned and expectant of the Westin experience that I thought we were in the wrong hotel—this one did not have the same pleasant fragrance as the others and it confused me.

This is the type of sensory detail you should transmit to your prospect when you're describing the ideal vacation you have found for them. How will they feel? What will they see, hear, and smell? How will this trip help them achieve their desired vacation experience?

Closing – get the credit card

As you are presenting the options you've identified for your prospect, watch and listen for signals: a head nod, affirmative verbalizations, or grunts and groans will let you know when it's time to ask for the credit card. Closing the sale can be both the easiest and hardest part of the whole process. This is the time when we must confront any fears and perceptions we may have about money and put them aside.

Most sales are lost for one simple reason: the sales person failed to ask for it. You may have put on the most incredible performance, emotionally connected with your prospect, and presented an unbelievable vacation package, but if you failed to ask for the credit card, you lose! And the potential customer loses, too, because they may not purchase their dream vacation.

Closing the sale means asking for payment. Either you get it or you don't, but you have to ask.

I have heard industry leaders and sales trainers tell their constituents that "you have to earn the right to close the sale." Not so, in my humble opinion. If a prospect reached out to you, whether solicited or otherwise, and asked you to research vacation options on their behalf with no guarantee of compensation, you *have* earned the right to ask for the sale. If you follow the system, asking for payment is just a natural step in the process. In fact, the customer expects you to do it. Hopefully, they are ready to buy at this point!

Answer objections – be a problem solver

But what if they have objections? That's fine. If you followed the process and asked lots of qualifying questions, you probably have answered most of their concerns along the way. Objections usually are not objections to your proposal. They are simply a request for more information. Objections may be based on perceptions or something they read on the internet. Perceptions may be real, but most are not, so it is our responsibility to make sure the prospect is fully informed.

For example, many people are reluctant to visit Dubai. I know I was before I visited. After all, it is in the Middle East—so it's not safe, they treat women poorly, you can't drink alcohol, and they only speak Arabic, right? Well, you can't change geography, so yes, it is in the Middle East. But other than that, Dubai is very different than most people perceive. It is an international destination, a modern-day Monaco, and it's one of the safest cities in the world. Most women dress in western clothing except when visiting mosques. Alcohol flows freely in restaurants and hotel bars, and everyone speaks English. In fact, even the street signs are in both Arabic and English. It is a very different destination than I originally perceived. This is the kind of education you can offer in response to objections that are based on flawed or limited perceptions.

Be prepared with answers to your own FAQs, questions you should expect from the prospect. If you are a cruise specialist, be prepared to answer questions about onboard product, hurricane season, motion sickness, and so on. If you specialize in a destination, you will be asked about local customs, appropriate dress, attractions, history, and dining, just to name a few.

Closing (repeat) – see above

One you have answered your prospect's questions and objections, repeat the closing. Yes, you have to ask for the credit card again. This time they'll feel more confident in their decision because you've answered all their questions and assuaged any fears. Congratulations! You made a sale!

Follow up – building relationships

Many types of purchases involve a lag time between the purchase decision and the actual product delivery. A homebuyer will place a deposit in escrow and pay the balance at closing—often with several months in between. The same is true with most vacation purchases. A deposit is made, followed by final payment sixty to ninety days prior to departure. As a salesperson, what you do in that time can make the difference in having a one-time sale or a long-term client.

Now that you have a customer, you don't want them to feel like a pumpkin. A key to building and maintaining your new relationship with your former prospect is the follow up, also known as service after the sale. Leading up to their purchase, you showered your prospect with attention. Now that she is a client or customer is not the time to let up. It is essential to have strategically placed touchpoints from the time of purchase until departure. There aren't rules for this, but you might want to establish a schedule of touchpoints for your business so your customers get a consistent level of service after the sale.

I'll give you an example. The first contact could be five days after purchase, perhaps an e-mail or phone call reminding them to buy travel insurance. Subsequent communication could verify dining and tour options, transfers and flights, and other trip option, and you should make one or two e-mails or calls saying, "Hey, just checking in. I know you are excited about your upcoming trip. Please remember I am here to be of service. Speaking of which, do you know anyone who would benefit from my services?"

The real work starts *after* the sale, and timely follow up is the key to success. Most travel agents will tell you they follow up with clients after they have returned from their trip, too. However, in my experience, their version of a follow up is often somewhat questionable. A voice mail or automated e-mail is not a good follow up. A good follow up will be either a live telephone conversation or personalized e-mail exchange asking what the client liked best and what they would change. This type of conversation shows the client you really care about them and their happiness with their vacation. You may not always want to hear them, but be sure to ask for candid comments on your service, too.

After the vacation follow up, it's not enough to just put the client back into the database to receive whatever targeted marketing is sent to them by you and your competitors. This is the biggest fail when comes to customer service. The key to retaining that customer is recency and frequency of contact—with you, not with a postcard or an e-mail. Recency and frequency is about building a long-term relationship with the customer—even when you are not trying to sell them anything. Customers will buy from the company that they hear from on a regular basis, but also the *last* one they heard from. Make sure that's you.

Ask for referrals – help me grow

If your customers are singing your praises, ask permission to post their comments about you on your website. These third party endorsements are invaluable. Now, if they have decided you ruined their entire vacation because you neglected to tell them in advance that the sun sets in the west, well—you might want to avoid their endorsement, and send them to your worst enemy in the business.

CALL TO ACTION PART 2

Now that you have a roadmap for the sales process, it's time to practice, practice, practice until you know your talking points backward and forward.

1. *Script your sales talk—or at least make a list of bullet points.* Now practice your sales talk in front of a mirror until your language feels

natural. Ideally, your prospect won't feel you are reciting a canned speech at them. It should flow like normal conversation.

2. *Find a willing guinea pig.* Call on your friends and family to play prospects. You can practice selling travel, or you can have fun with it and sell them the salt and pepper shakers on the dining room table. It doesn't matter what you're selling when you role play. What matters is that you're following the process.

3. *Make a plan for how you'll follow up with customers.* If you have a schedule of touchpoints planned in advance, it will be simple to provide excellent service after the sale.

4. *Use dynamic prospecting to reach out to previous customers for referrals.* Do you already have a number of satisfied customers? If you haven't recently, reach out to them for referrals. This is a great way to build your list of prospects and grow your business.

Chapter 5
Why Travel Agents Fail

There's a phrase I've been throwing around in this book and maybe you don't believe me. "It's easy!" or "it's simple!" You're probably thinking, *if it's so easy, Dan, then why do so many travel agents fail?* That's a fair question. Plenty of smart, skilled agents don't make it in our business. Why is that? I've identified some key reasons that travel professionals fail and I'll share them with you—so you can bulletproof your business against them.

As a sales coach and business adviser, the question I am asked most often is, "What do I have to do to become successful?" It is a simple question and one that really has a simple answer.

Contrary to popular belief, the reason many travel agents fail is not due to lack of product knowledge, lack of planning, or lack of marketing. In fact, we tend to be pretty good at all three. The cost of entry in travel sales is typically very low, so it's usually not for lack of funding either.

No, the reason many agents fail is so obvious that it is often overlooked. According to legendary management consultant Peter Drucker, "the purpose of a business is to create and keep customers." That's it—period. Nothing else happens in this or any business until someone buys something. This first sale generates the revenue to help keep the lights and internet on. It helps to create momentum and funds marketing initiatives. This sale, and the others that will follow, help you to create the lifestyle you want for you and your family. But it all starts with a single sale—or does it?

Actually, it starts much sooner. In the travel business, it is common vernacular to refer to everyone as a "client." However, in the sales profession, the proper use of the words "client" and "customer" refer to those who have actually purchased a product or service. All others are called "prospects." This is not a chicken or the egg debate. The path is quite clear: before someone becomes a client, they must first be a prospect. *So the real reason many travel agents fail is not due to a lack of clients, but to a lack of prospects.*

Prospecting can be a scary thing. To many salespeople, it is synonymous with cold-calling. However, this is just one of many prospecting techniques, so let's think of prospecting in terms we can all relate to—fishing. I haven't met too many folks that don't enjoy fishing.

Let's say you decide to go fishing one day and are pretty sure there are hundreds of fish in the pond you choose. You have set a goal of catching three fish, all keepers. You spend the day casting your line with just the right bait, putting it right under the nose of the fish as they swim across the pond. You get some nibbles and a few you thought were "on hook," but they got away. You reeled a couple in but threw them back as they were too small. And then there are the keepers, the ones you can take home. You are feeling pretty good about them because you will be able to eat for a few days. In a nutshell, this is what prospecting is all about.

There are hundreds of fish (prospects) out there just waiting to be caught. You have to cast your line numerous times, putting your lure right in front of them until one bites. Some will be will become keepers (customers), and others will get off the hook. That's OK because there are more fish in the pond, and they will bite when the time is right. Without prospects, you don't have customers, and without customers, you don't have revenue. Without revenue, you don't eat. So the key is to always keep restocking your pond.

But Dan, what about my marketing plan? Isn't this supposed to attract prospects? In this context, marketing is part of what's called an attraction strategy. Assuming you are executing the activities in your plan, most marketing programs are reactive, meaning the prospect initiates the sales conversation. It's a lot like fishing with a bobber instead of a lure. You pick a spot, throw it out your line, hoping to attract a fish with your offer of a worm at the end of the line. It sits there until a fish comes along and decides whether or not to bite. Depending on how long it has been sitting in the water, the worm might be old and unattractive so the fish may not bite.

If your prospecting strategy is your marketing plan, you probably don't get many calls. Don't get me wrong, marketing is a very important part of your overall business strategy. However, marketing and prospecting are very different disciplines. Prospecting, like cast fishing, is a proactive process conducted with systematic precision. The most successful travel agents are salespeople and the most successful salespeople in any profession are good—no, *great* prospectors.

When I talk to agents in the field, at conferences, and tradeshows, most of them tell me how they are struggling to make it. They tend to blame the economy, the weather, clients (remember, until they buy, they should be referred to as prospects), suppliers, host, consortia, the dog, and so on for their lack of sales. The only one they don't blame is themselves. So I ask this simple question: "How many calls have you made to your prospects?"

When people complain that "sales is not easy," they don't usually mean the process of selling. This in itself is actually quite fun when you think about it. No, when they complain about "sales," they really mean "prospecting is not easy."

Ask any sales person their least favorite part of the job and they will be the first to tell you it's prospecting. Professional sales people, even those who are the most successful at what they do, know if they do not prospect on a daily basis, they will not be eating in next sixty to ninety days.

In sales, we often hear the phrase "keep the funnel full." But what does that really mean? Remember, a funnel is shaped like an upside-down cone with a hole in the bottom. You pour in a large amount of stuff and some of it comes out below. Sales people refer to it as a funnel because you begin with a large number of prospects and through a series of touches and processes, a small steady stream of customers comes out the other end.

As small-business people, we wear a number of hats, from CEO to janitor. The most important hat you wear is that of "Chief Sales Officer," because your sales efforts provide the means for the other roles to exist.

I teach my clients to focus on the fundamentals. There are a lot of programs and apps that claim social media and automation will drive the sales process for you so you can sit back and watch the customers line up to buy your stuff. There are many that will help you become more efficient, but the folks selling these programs have their own agendas and if they can do what they claim, why do they ask for your phone number?

As much as these companies claim to be able to solve your prospecting problem by automating the sales process, they understand that *people buy from people*. This means picking up the phone and having a conversation with their prospects. They don't call it "dialing for dollars" for nothing. It works.

The more people you can talk to about your product, the more quotes, presentations, and sales you will make. The numbers don't lie. This is how you keep your sales funnel full and a steady stream of commission checks in your bank account.

But Dan, I don't have time for this—I have so much other stuff to do. I know, and it is easy to get distracted, so let me be crystal clear: this is the most important thing you can do for your business. You must prioritize prospecting.

Initially, block an hour or two in the morning for prospecting calls, e-mails, and social-media posts. Do not allow interruptions. You must protect this time as though it were a meeting with your most important customer because this is exactly what it is.

You will get rejected. You will be cursed, yelled at, have the phone slammed in your ear. No way to sugar coat it—rejection is hard. No matter what, even the best of us take some of it personally. But you will also be profusely thanked, invited into homes, and have the wonderful opportunity to provide a valuable service for your prospect by helping them with one of their most valuable assets, one they highly covet—their vacation experience.

Here is the simple secret to your success. *Everything* you do must be designed to get a customer. Your website, marketing activities, social media, e-mail, and phone conversations are all tools which should support your proactive, outbound prospecting efforts. They are tools to help attract and drive prospects into the funnel. You are responsible for your own success and proactive prospecting is the key.

There is an old saying in the sales profession: "Always Be Closing." In my opinion, closing the sale is one of the easiest parts of the process—as long as you have the courage to ask for the credit card. The real challenge is prospecting, which is why "Always Be Prospecting" is my mantra! If you keep a steady flow of prospects, you should never run out of customers. This is the real reason why some people are consistently top sellers and become Wealthy Travel Agents!

APPENDIX

GLOSSARY OF ACRONYMS

AAA	American Automobile Association
AARP	American Association of Retired Persons
BS	your garden-variety bullshit
C.R.A.P.	criticism, rejection, assholes, pressure—stuff you don't need in your life!
CAA	Canadian Automobile Association
CEO	chief executive officer
CRM	customer relationship management
CTC	certified travel consultant or, if you are the boss, chief toilet cleaner
FAM	familiarization trip—an educational trip to learn product or destination firsthand
FAQ	frequently asked questions
FIT	fully or foreign independent traveler
GP	general practitioner
IC	independent contractor
IRS	Internal Revenue Service
KIA	know-it-all
LTV	lifetime value

MLM	multi-level marketing
NASA	National Aeronautics and Space Administration
OSM	oh shit moment
PATH	Professional Association of Travel Hosts
POS	point of sale
S.H.I.P.	skills, habits, inspiration, and performance: the four components of your success!
S.W.A.G.	scientific wild-ass guess
SBC	shipboard credit
VTG	Vacations To Go
WTA	Wealthy Travel Agent
ZOPA	zone of opportunity for agreement

RECOMMENDED READING LIST

General Business

The E-Myth Revisited by Michael Gerber
Middle Class Millionaire by Lewis Schiff and Russ Alan
   Prince
The Millionaire Mentor by Greg Reid
The Millionaire Next Door by Dr. Thomas Stanley
The Millionaire Real Estate Agent by Gary Keller
REWORK by Jason Fried and David Heinemeier
   Hansson
*Wooden on Leadership: How to Create a Winning
   Organization* by John Wooden

Self-Help

The Art of Exceptional Living by Jim Rohn
Lead the Field by Earl Nightingale
The Power of Habits by Charles Duhigg
The Power of Now by Eckerd Tolle
The War of Art by Steven Pressfield
The Way We Are Working Isn't Working by Tony
   Schwartz

Marketing and Sales

Book Yourself Solid by Michael Port
Contagious: Why Things Catch On by Jonah Burger
How to Sell Anything to Anybody by Joe Girard
It's Not Who You Know, But Who Knows You by David
  Arvin
Let Them Eat Cake by Pam Danziger
Marketing to the Affluent by Dr. Thomas Stanley

ABOUT THE AUTHOR

Dan Chappelle is a successful entrepreneur and top sales professional in the Travel and Tourism industries. In 1993, he started a travel company that became one of the top cruise sellers in North America at the time. After selling the company, he gave corporate life a shot, holding executive leadership roles within the Carlson Leisure Group (now Travel Leaders), Expedia CruiseShipCenters, and most recently Windstar Cruises, where he served as Vice President of Travel Agency, Charters and Incentives, and International Sales. His sales team played a key role in transforming Windstar Cruises into Conde Nast's 2014 World's Best Small Ship Cruise Line.

Dan left corporate life behind in 2015 to fulfill a long-time passion of helping others achieve success in travel sales. This desire became the catalyst for the Wealthy Travel Agent Academy, a coaching and training firm focused on developing sales leaders in the travel and tourism verticals. His no-nonsense approach has quickly made him a favorite in organizations both large and small.

Dan lives in the Seattle area with his wife, three designer dogs, two cats, and one grand-cat (those of you who have one know what this means). He has three beautiful daughters and is an avid hiker, occasional mountain climber, scuba instructor, and rabid University of Georgia Bulldogs fan.

Learn more at **www.DanChappelle.com**

What People are saying about S.H.I.P.

"From mindset to strategy and everything in between, this is a textbook on succeeding in the travel industry from someone who has done it. It will benefit both the seasoned travel advisor or someone new to the business providing a blueprint on how to do it right. As a sales/business coach myself, this is a must-have in any library!"

"Wow! I just finished reading Dan Chappelle's BOOK! GET YOUR S.H.I.P TOGETHER!. Best read I've had for some time! From the first page he had me. It's an easy read with a no-nonsense, real and to-the-point take the world of sales that he shares with you every step of the way. I saw myself in his scenarios and after 18 years in the Travel Industry and stepping out on my own THE SKY'S THE LIMIT! I'm excited to see what the future holds with these new insights, tools and practices that I have learned from Dan and his excellent book! He also made me laugh out loud with some of his insights and writing style. If you really want to learn how to grow your business and find value in yourself like never before READ THIS TODAY! It's truly amazing how he makes you see how easy it can be if you just break it down! It has found it's own special spot on my desk for days when I might need that little "adjustment"."

"Dan's book was a win for me, a win for my team, and a win for the franchise partners we serve at ECSC. ALL travel and cruise professionals will benefit from his insight and tried and tested wisdom - I know I did after 20+years selling, training, coaching and leading sales teams. The book easily reads to assist dedicated sellers of cruise and travel to grow, specialize, and thrive in the

21 Century of travel. Use this book, especially chapter 5, to gain your share of the $1.6 trillion dollar global travel market."

"I love this book! Dan's non-nonsense, straightforward and affable approach have made this book a must have resource for my office and my team. The strategies and resources he provides have helped me hone in and monetize on my unique offering, allowing me unlimited potential to grow my business and my brand."

"Attended a seminar where Dan spoke and I was able to get his book. I read it it on the flight home! Super easy read and provided a wealth of information. I am a seasoned travel agent of over 35 years and it was extremely helpful in helping figure out how to work smarter (not harder). I am looking forward to the next year to see a huge shift in my income!!!"

"If you are serious about being a successful Travel Agent this book will get you there. I have been in the travel industry for over 30 years and found the information very helpful. I am buying a copy for all my employees."

"Dan's book is a very valuable resource for the new and experienced travel advisor. I found it a useful reminder of some things I knew and a great eye opener for things I didn't know. A recommended read!"

GET YOUR S.H.I.P. TOGETHER!

Made in the USA
Columbia, SC
02 July 2024

37874002R00096